CONEY ISLAND WATERDANCE

PETER KAYAFAS

Coney Island Waterdance

PURPLE MARTIN PRESS   NEW YORK   2021

For Nancy Lassalle

*They landed at Coney, and were dashed on the crest of
a great human wave of mad pleasure-seekers into the walks
and avenues of Fairyland gone into vaudeville.*

—O. HENRY, FROM 'BRICKDUST ROW'

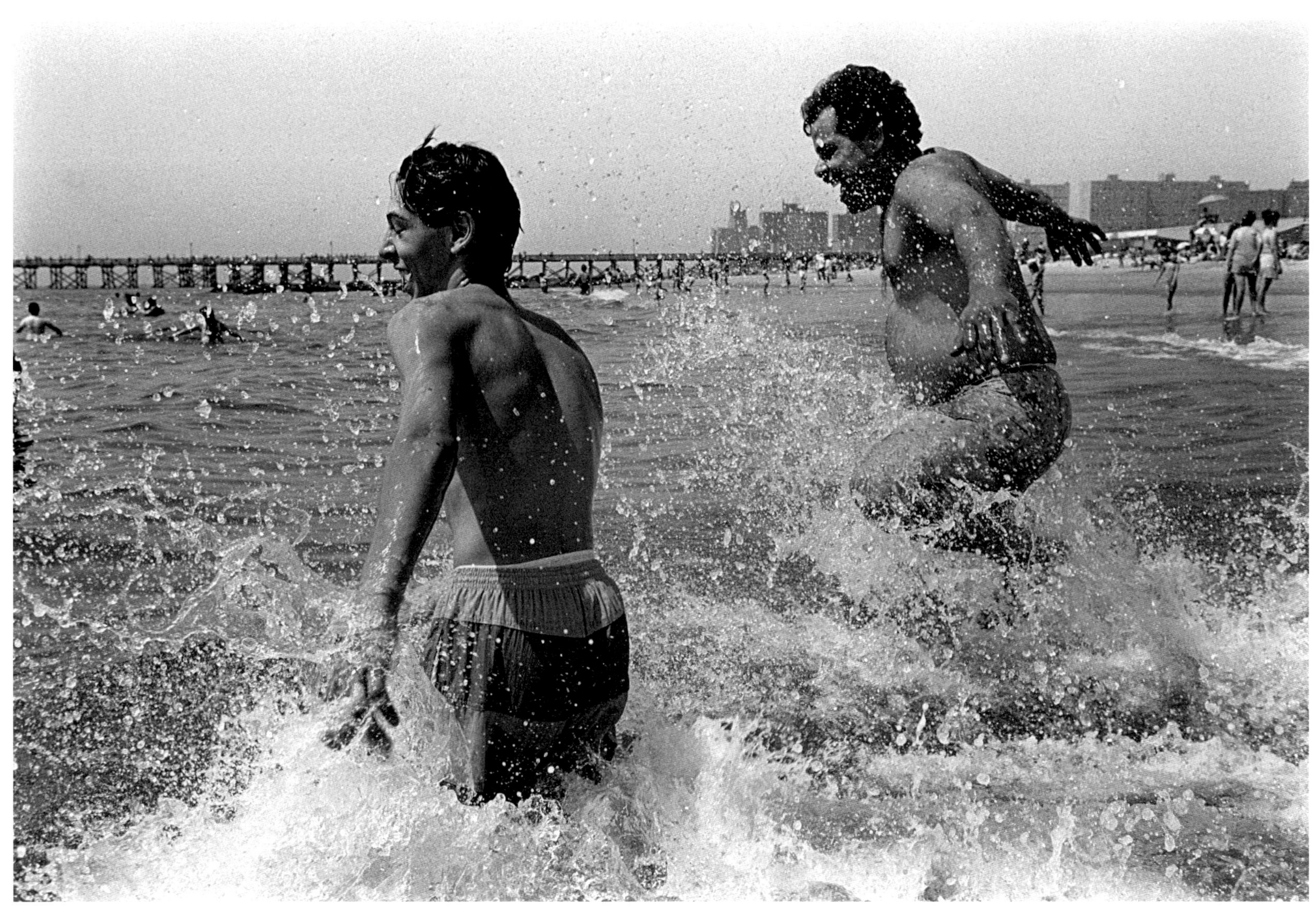

1.

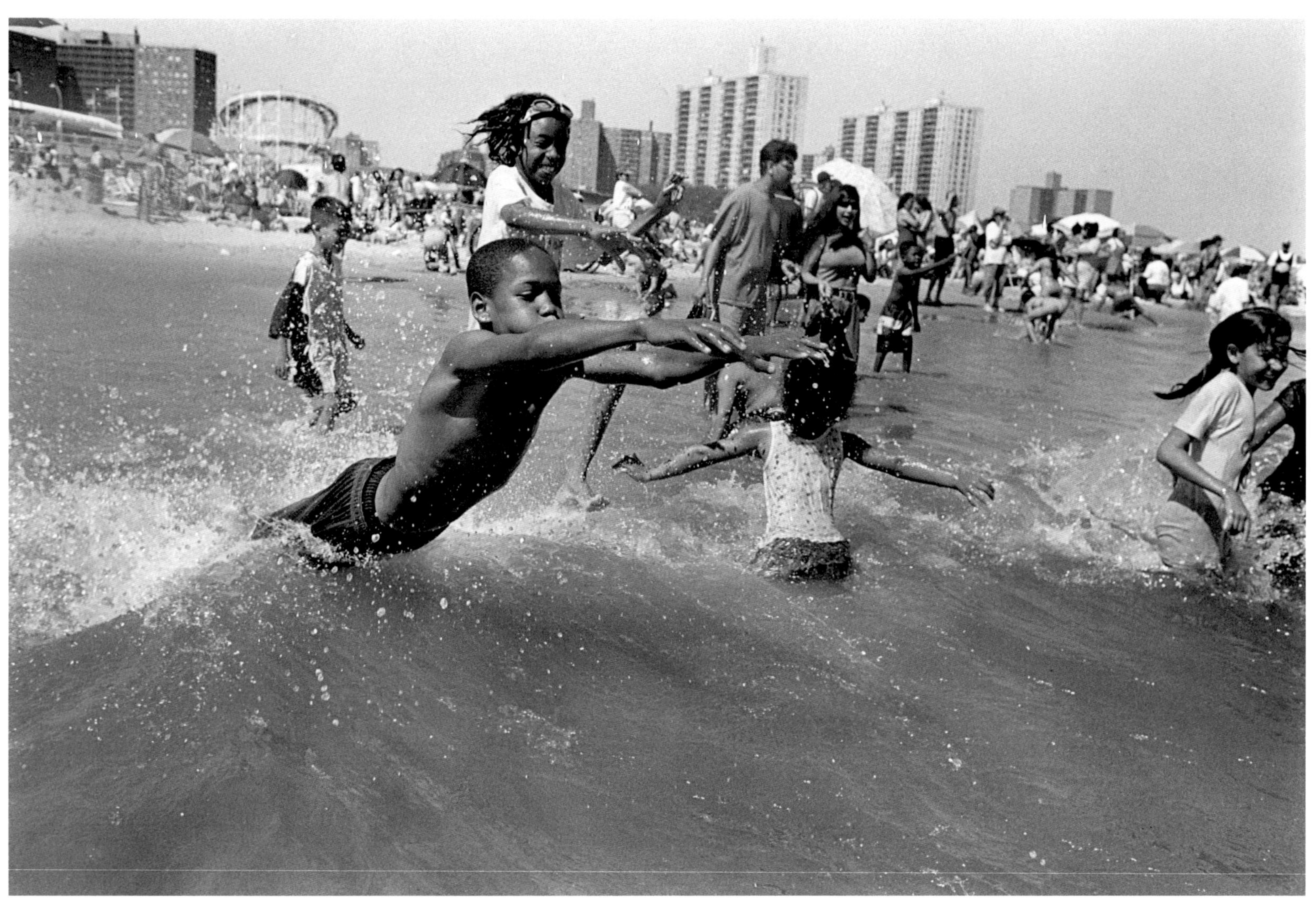

2.

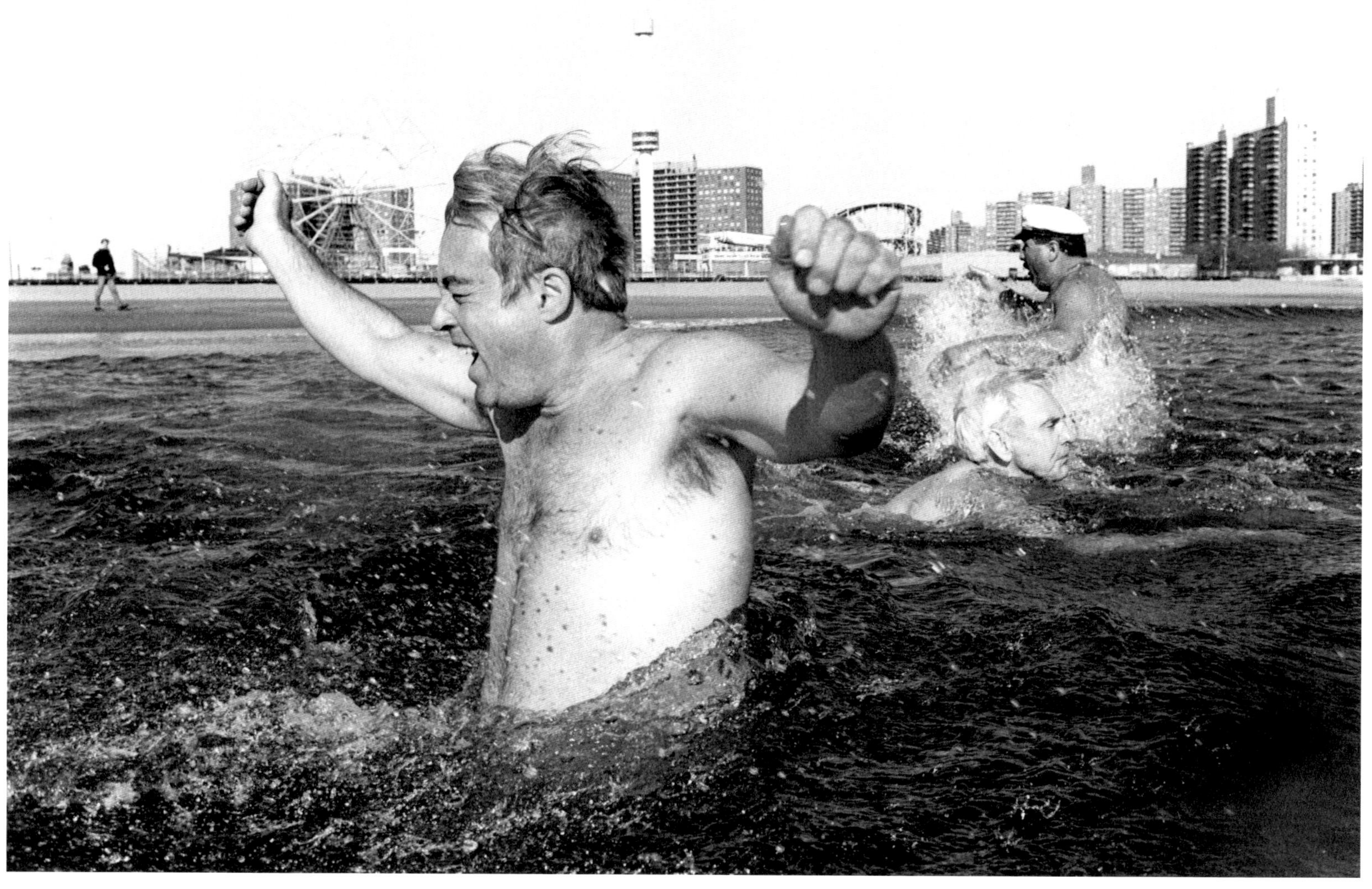

3.

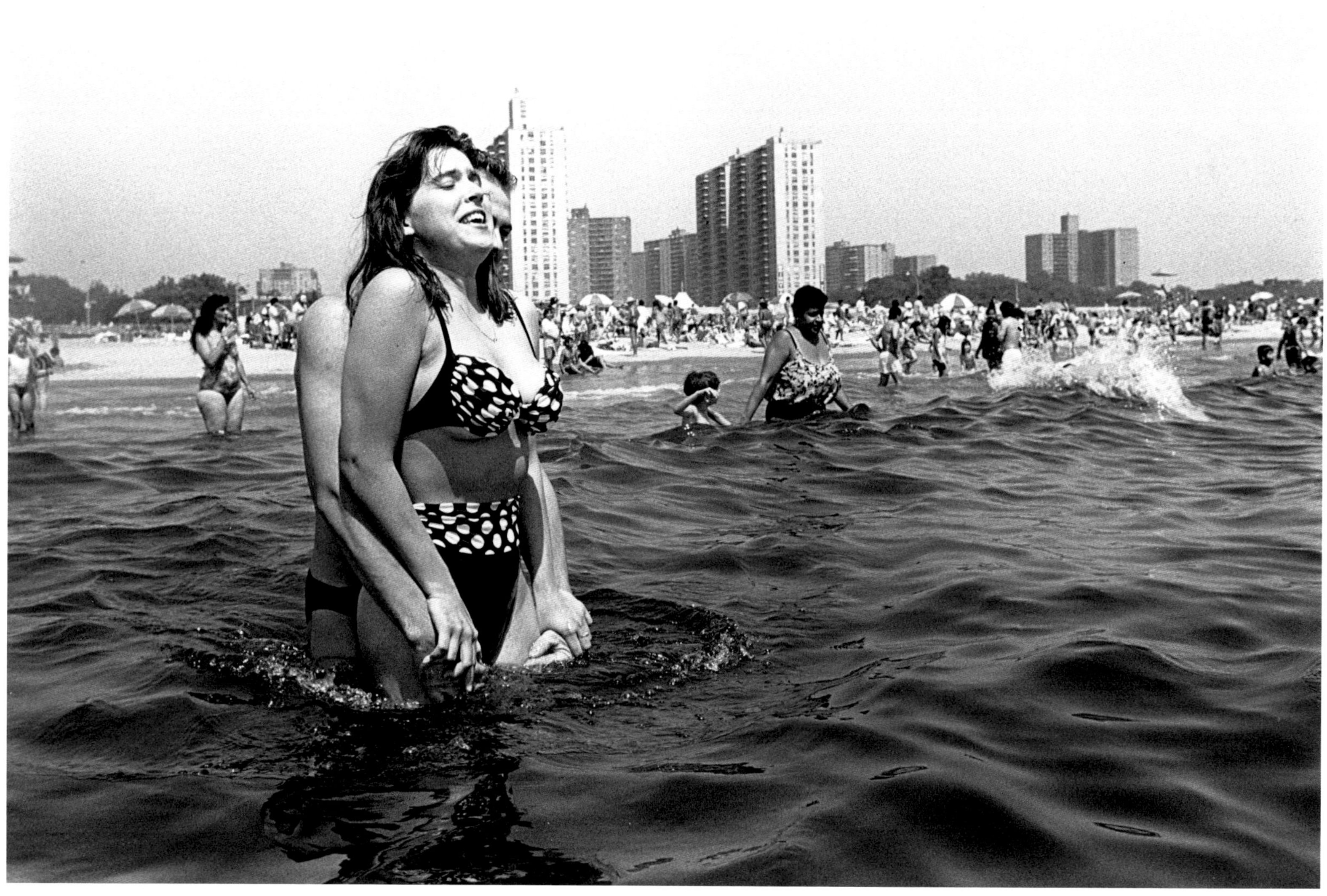

4.

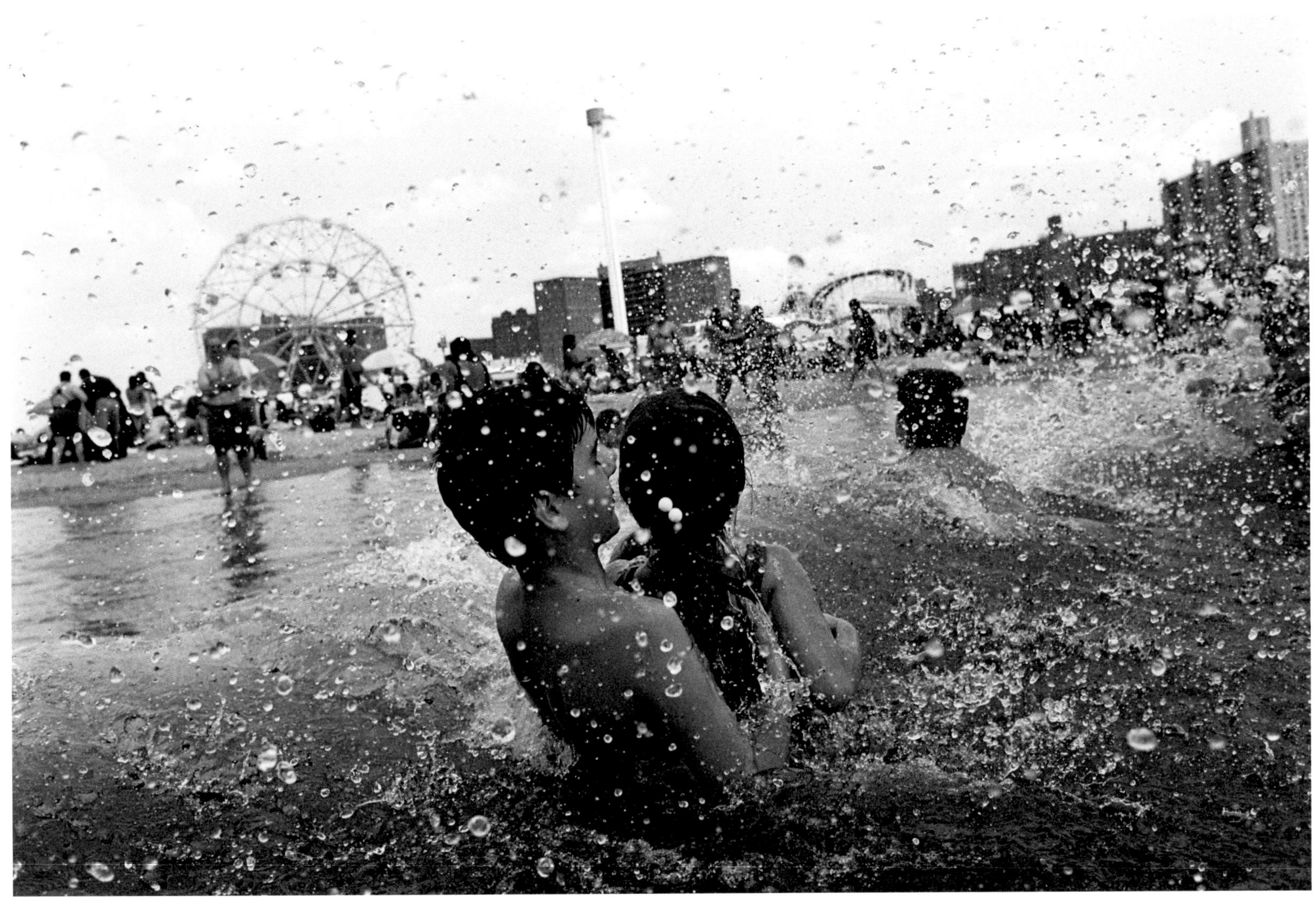

5.

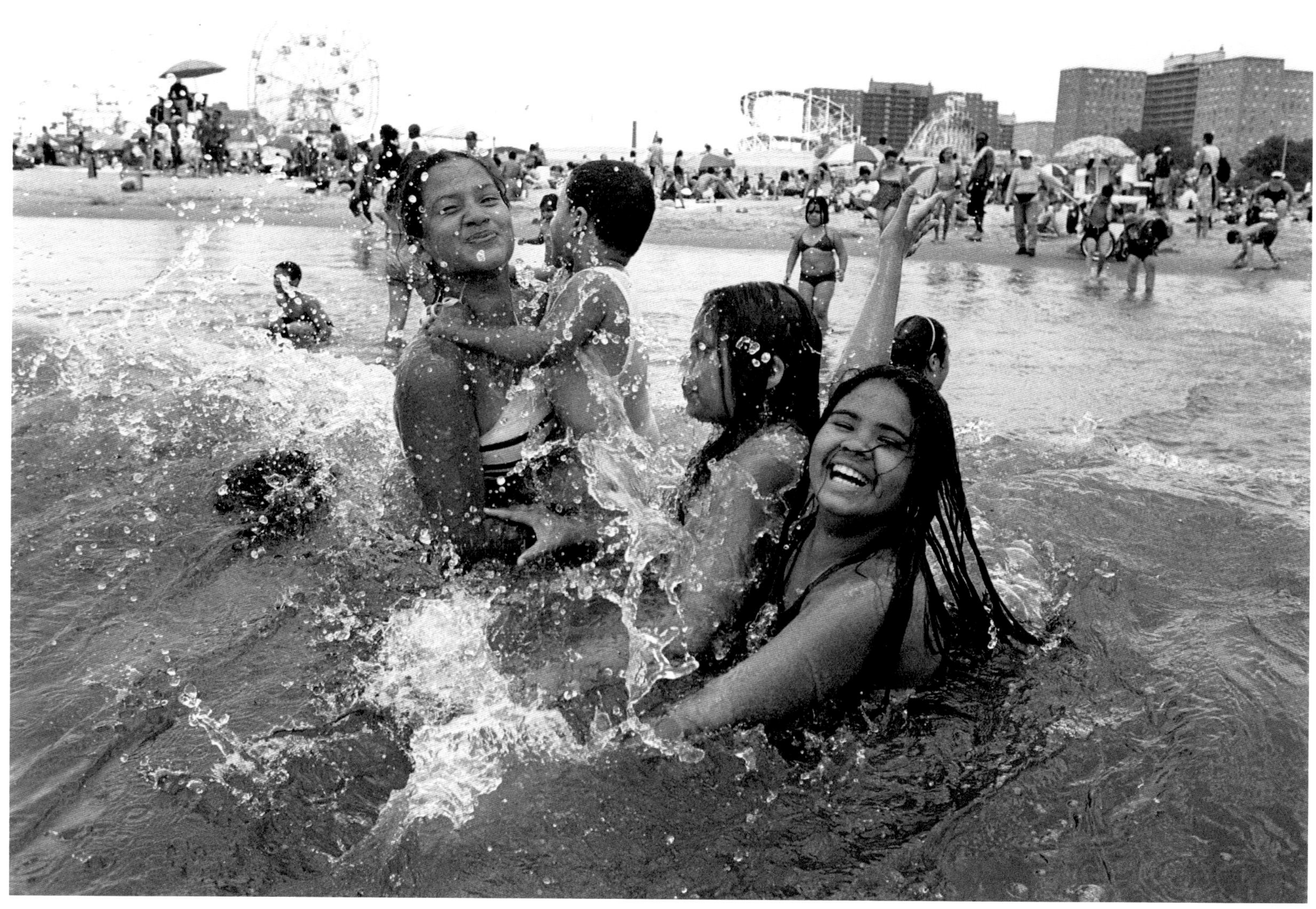

6.

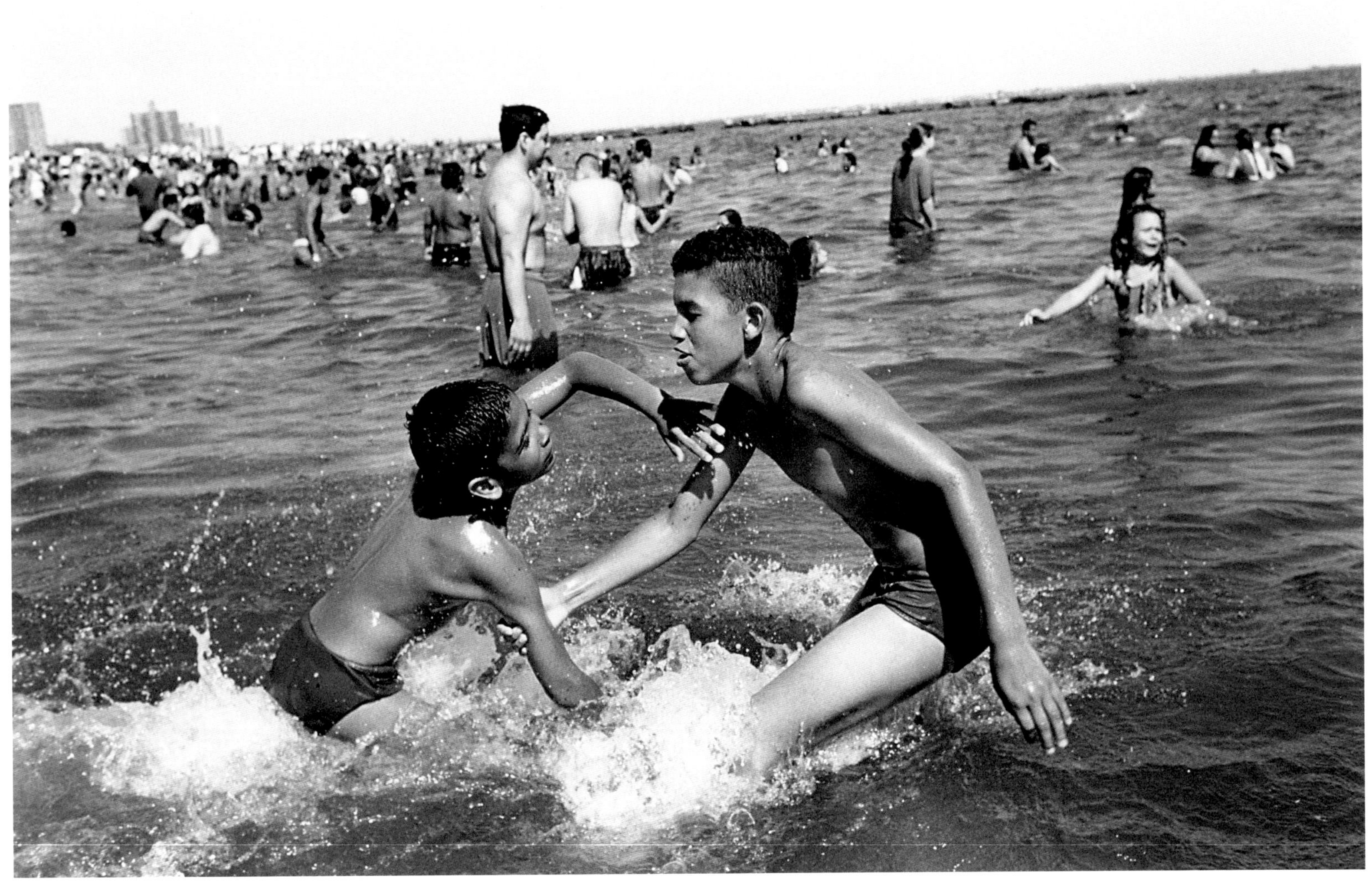

7.

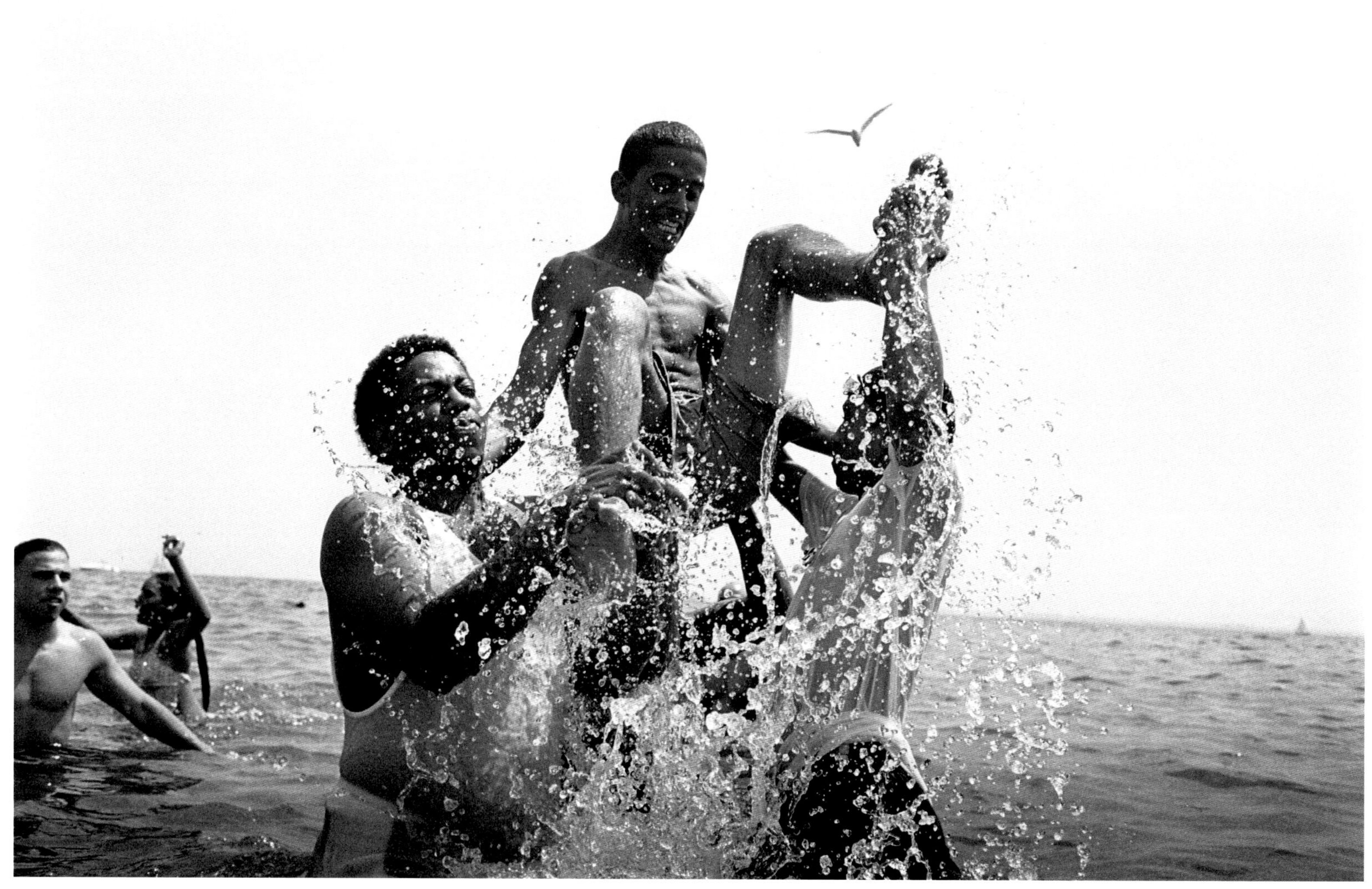

8.

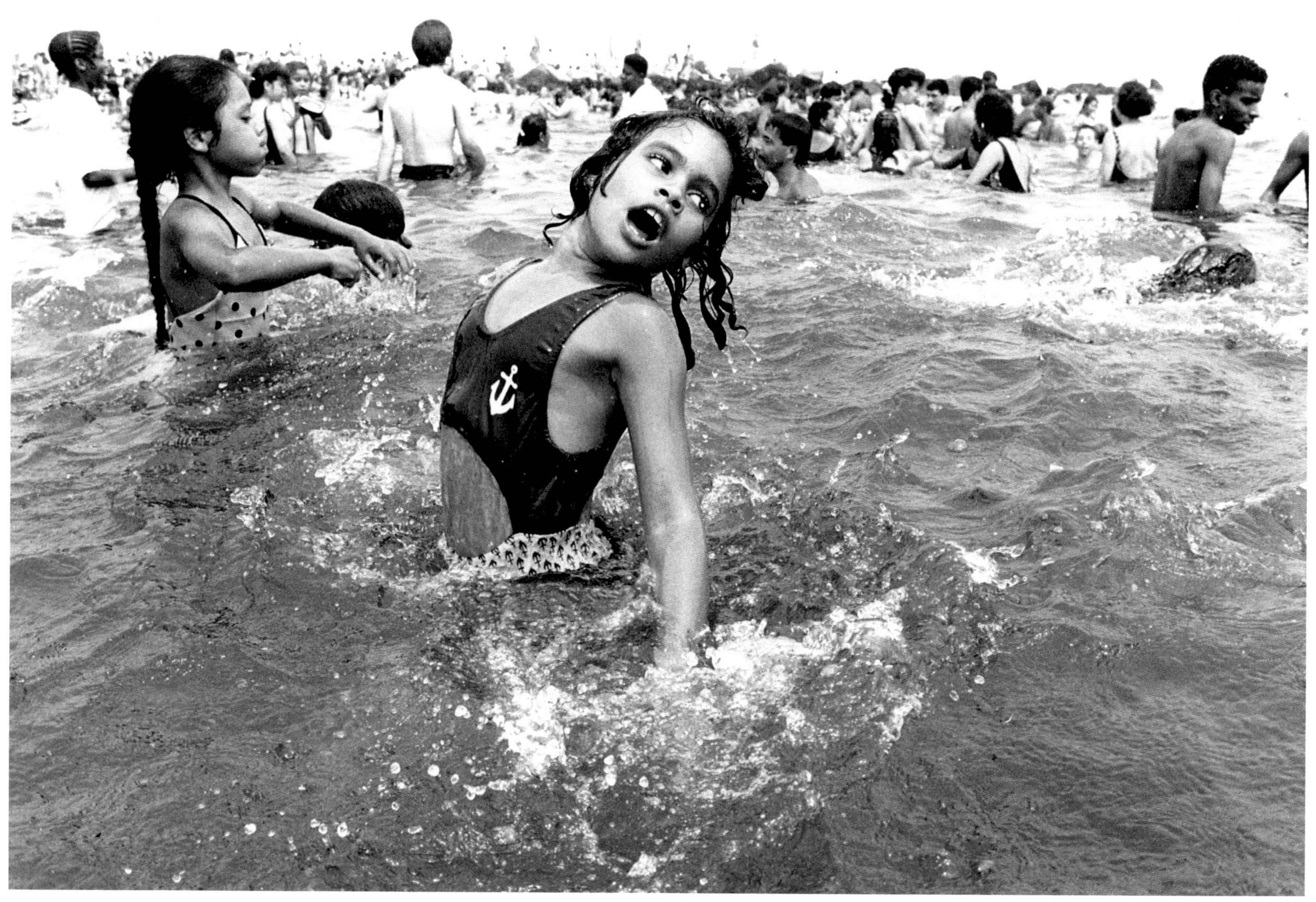

9.

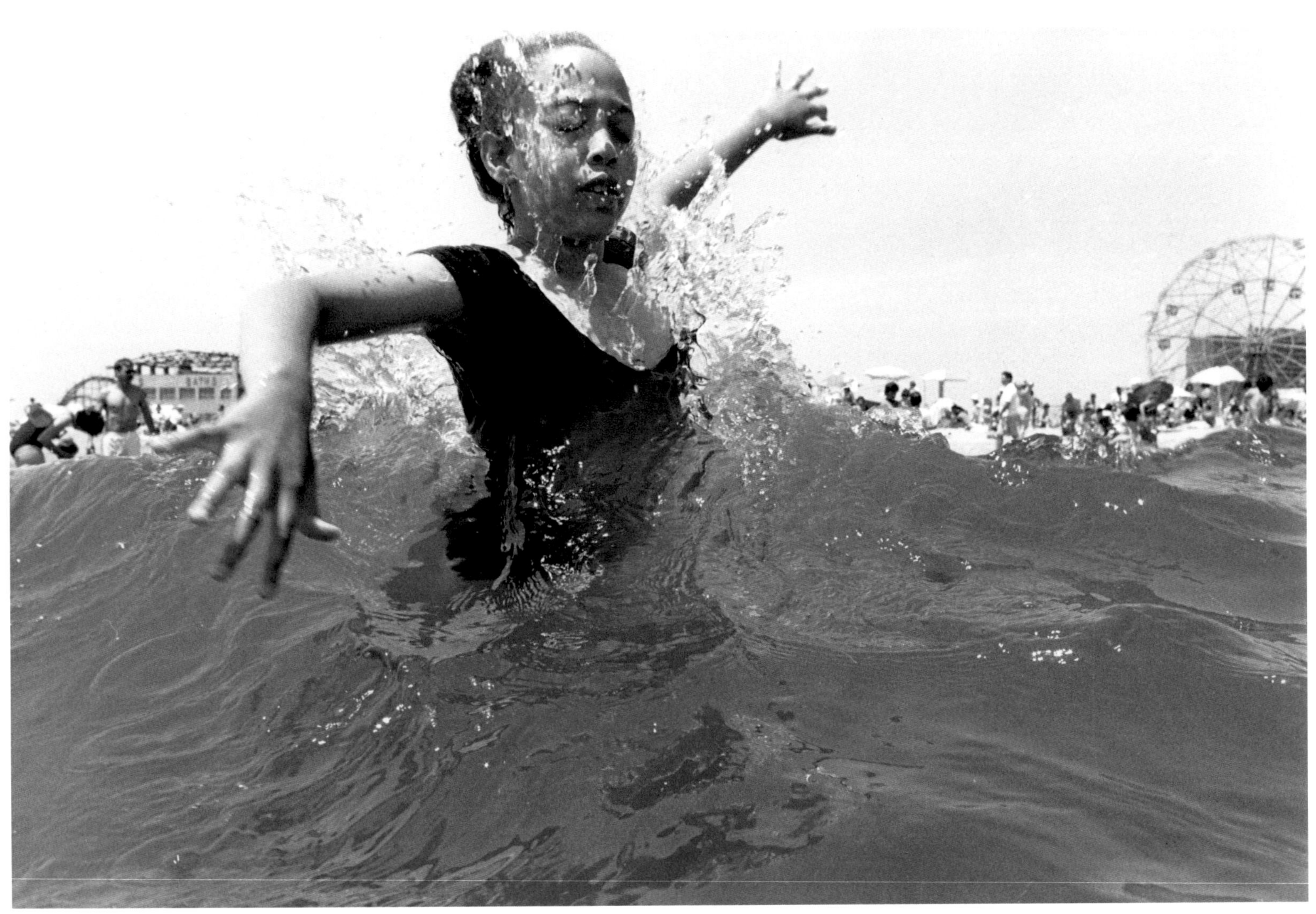

10.

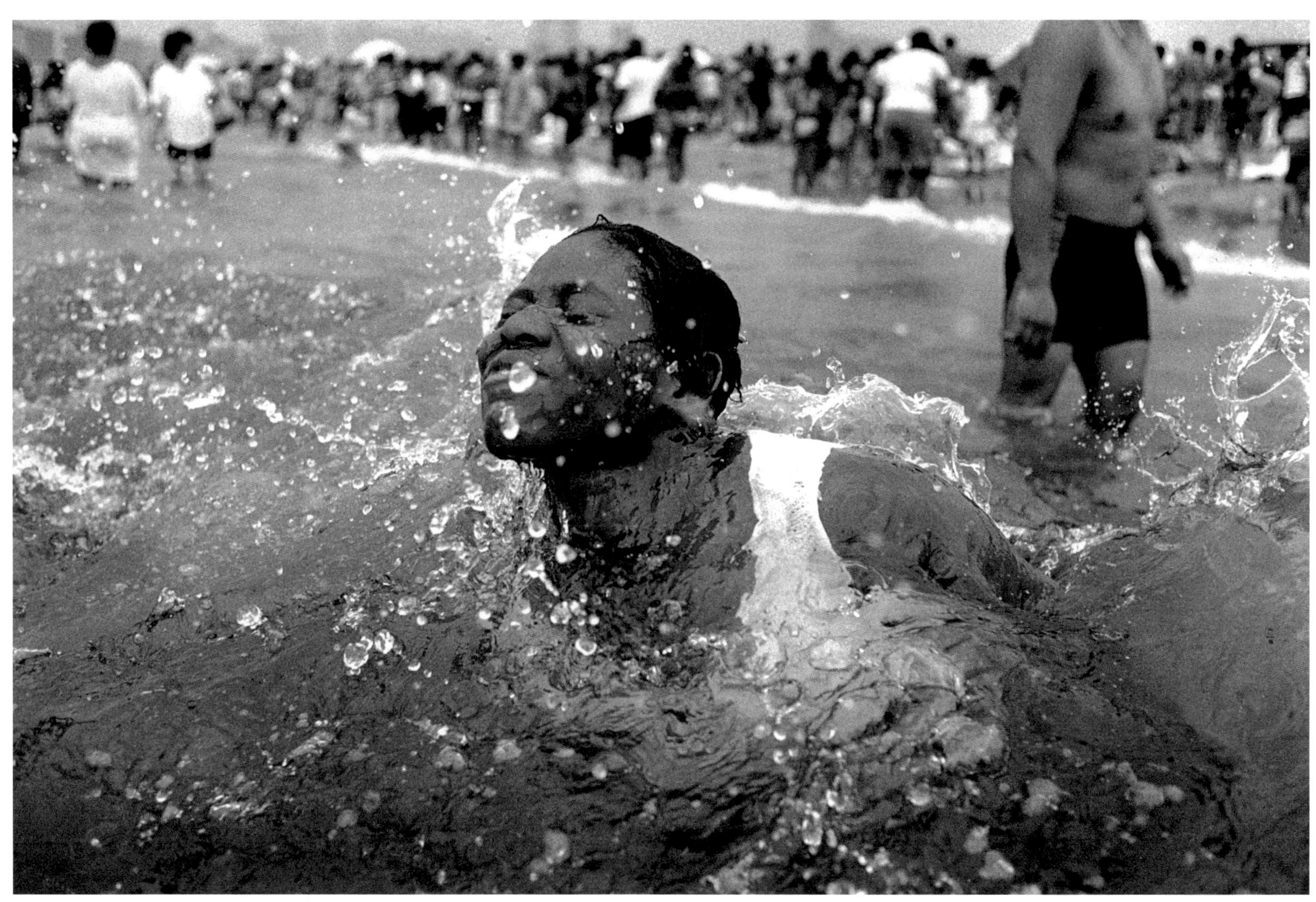

11.

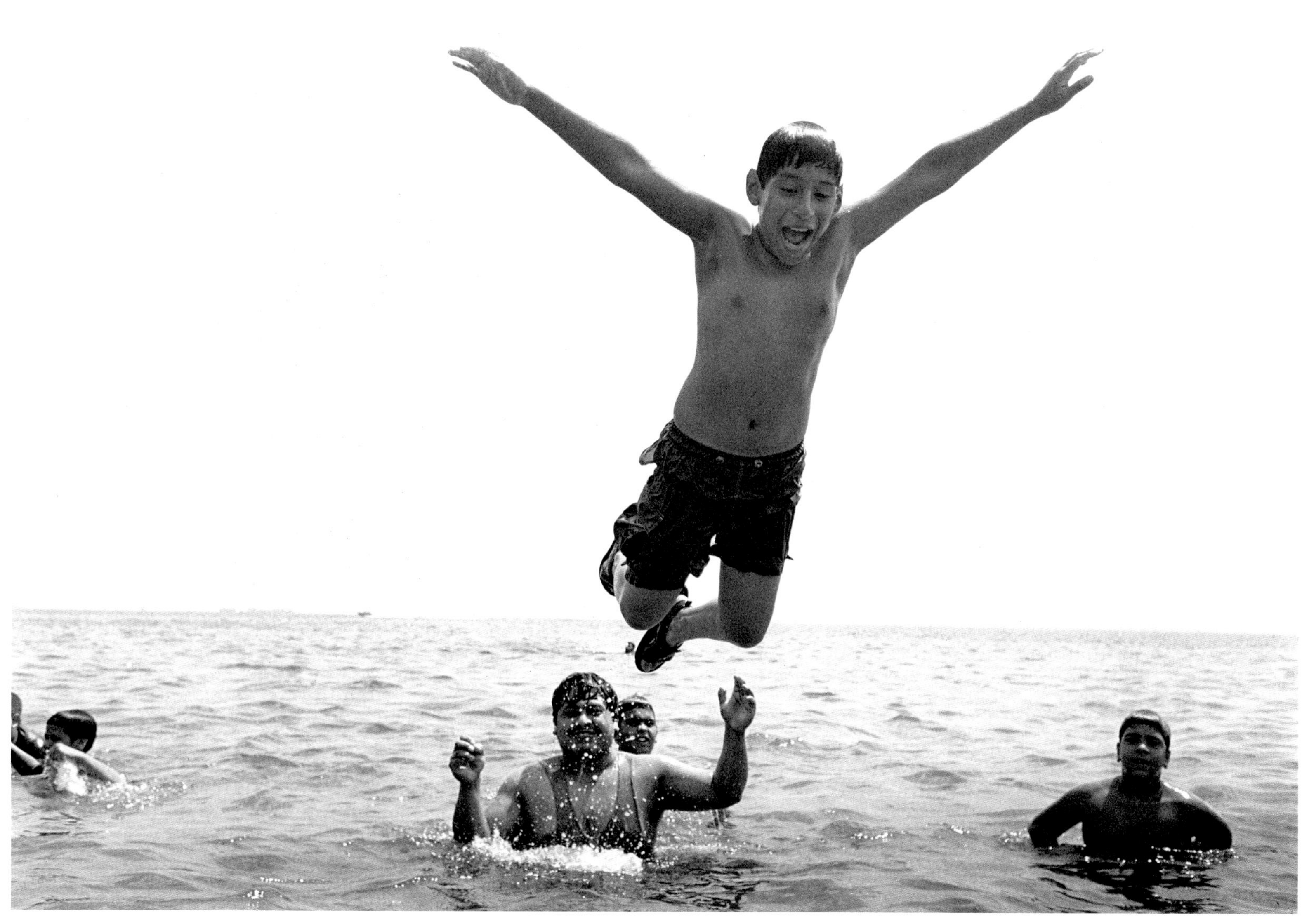

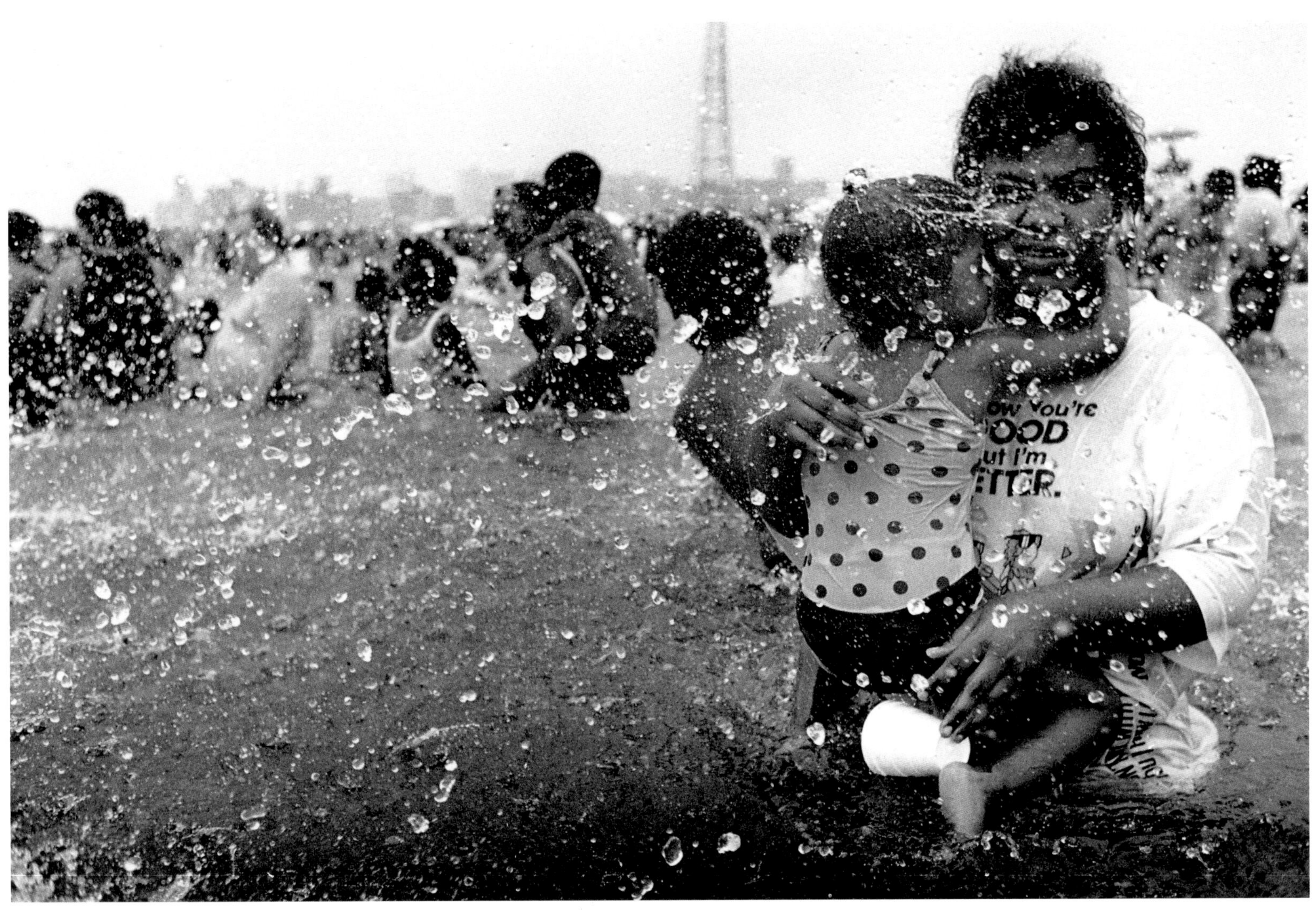

13.

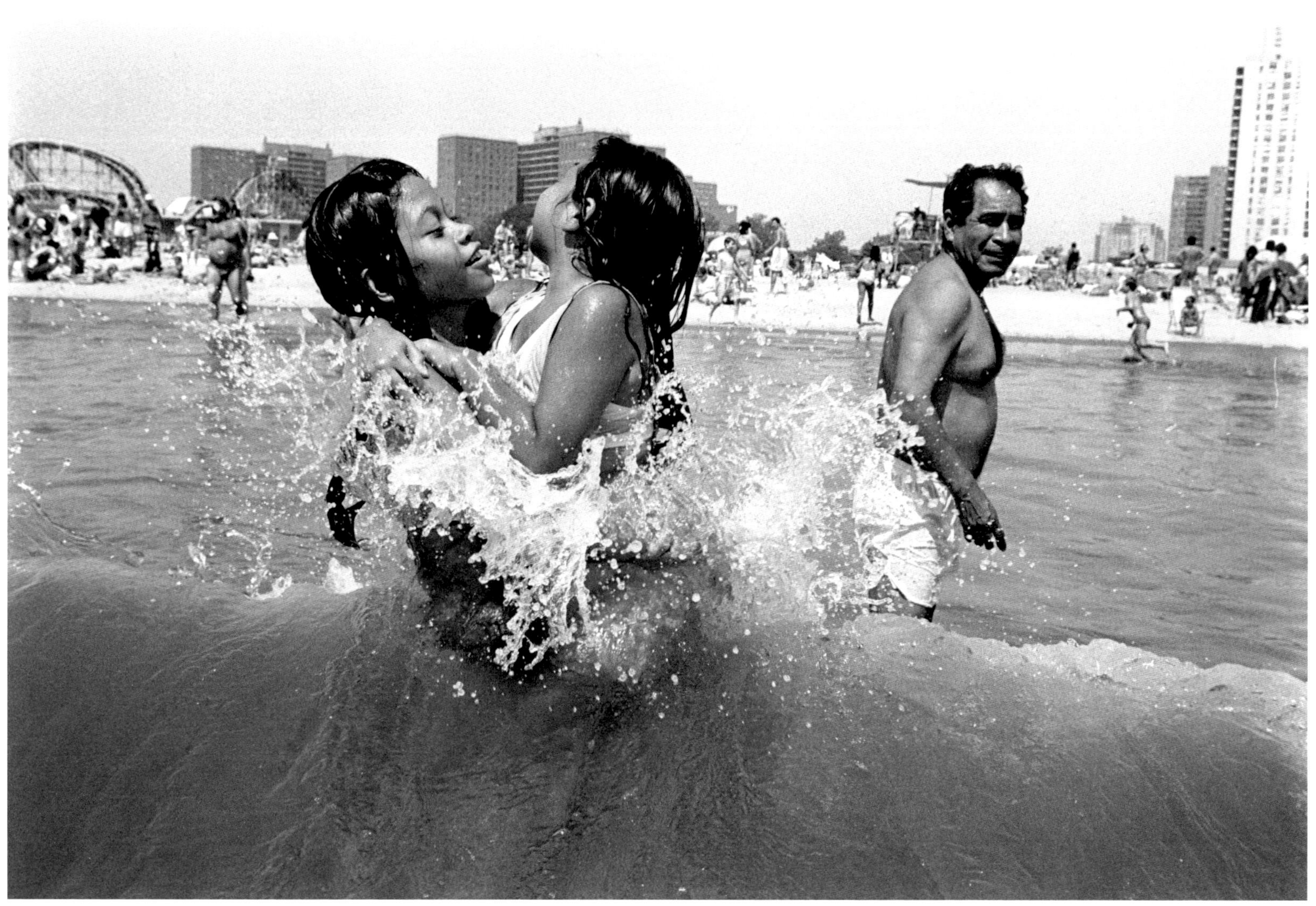

14.

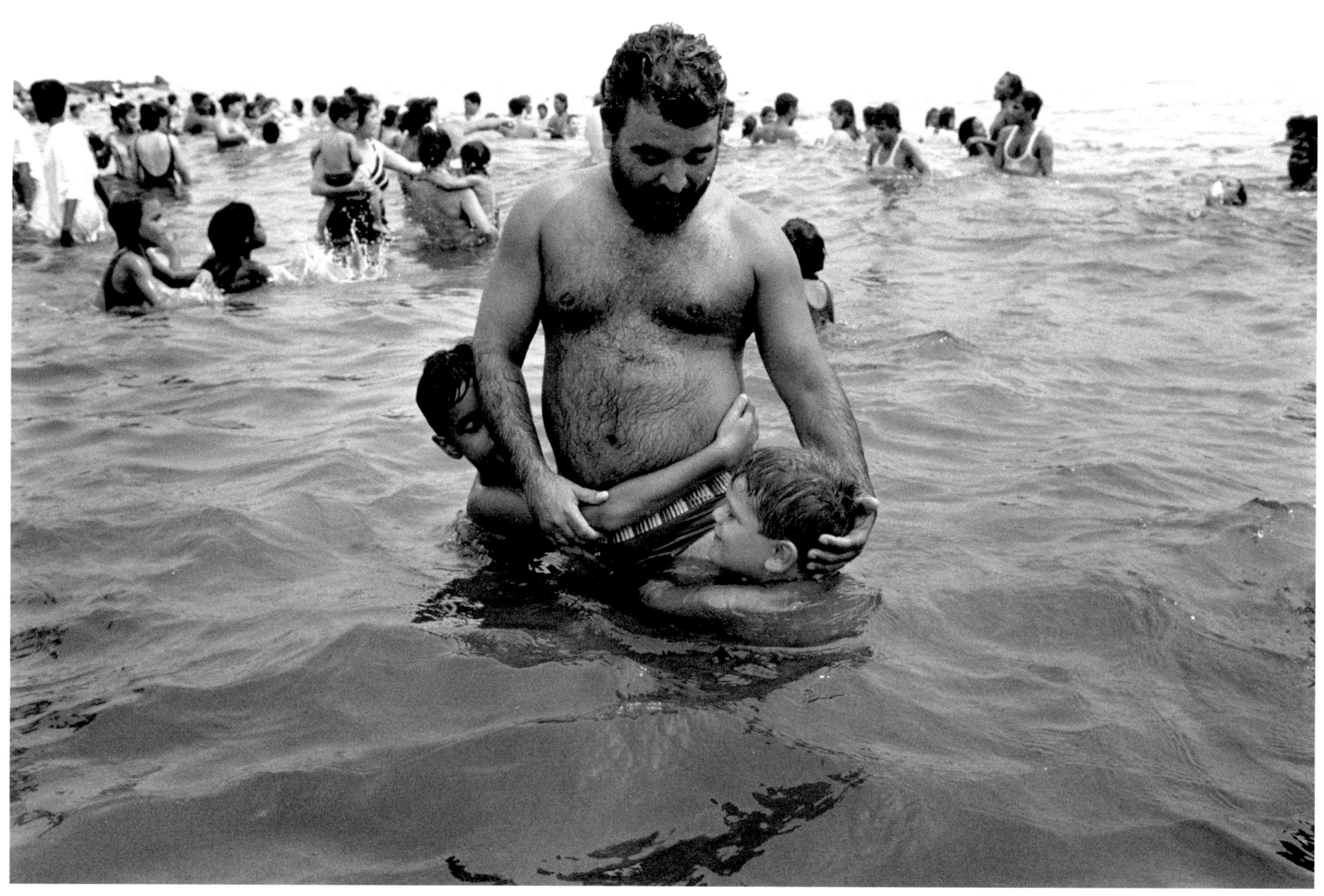

15.

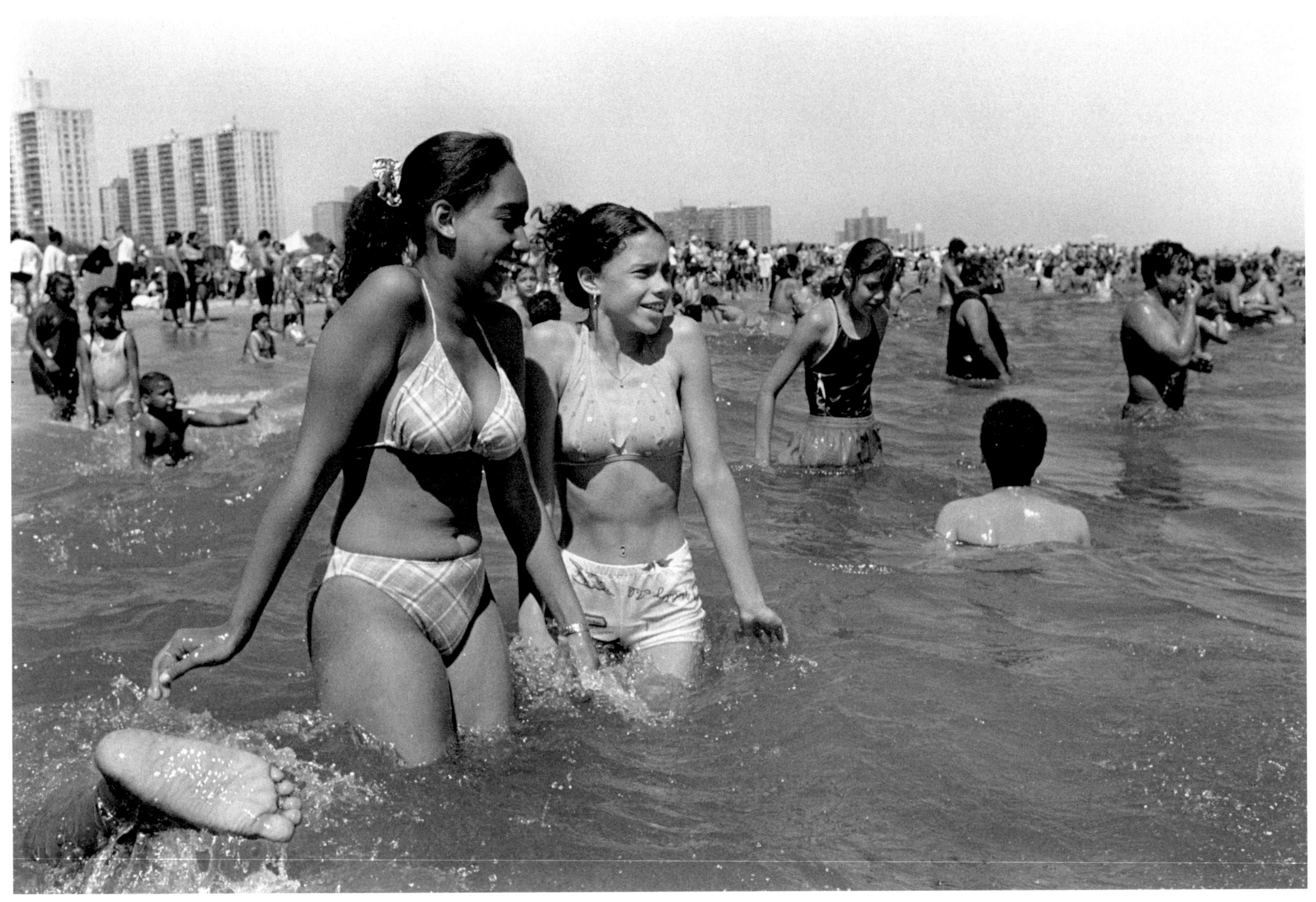

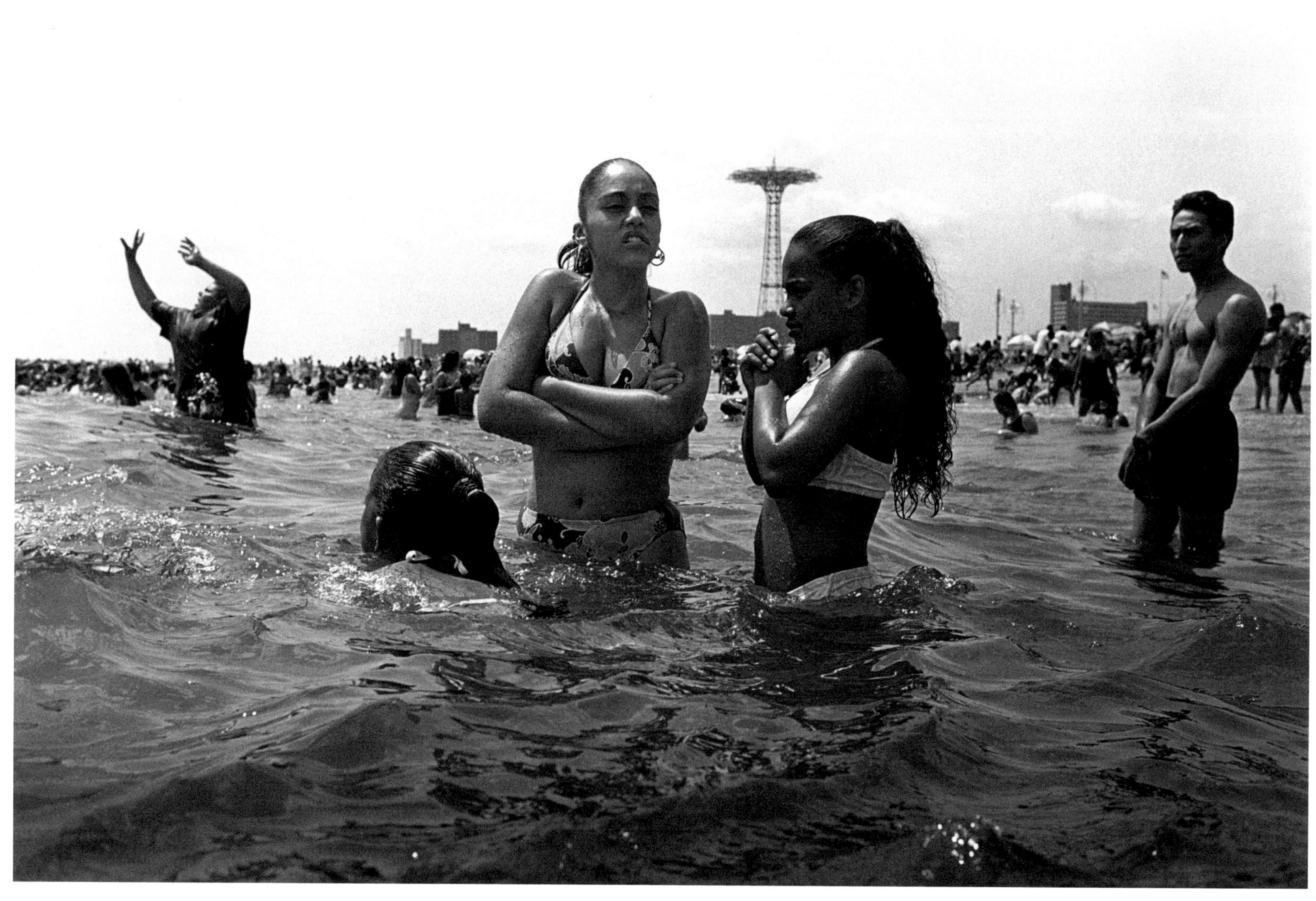

17.

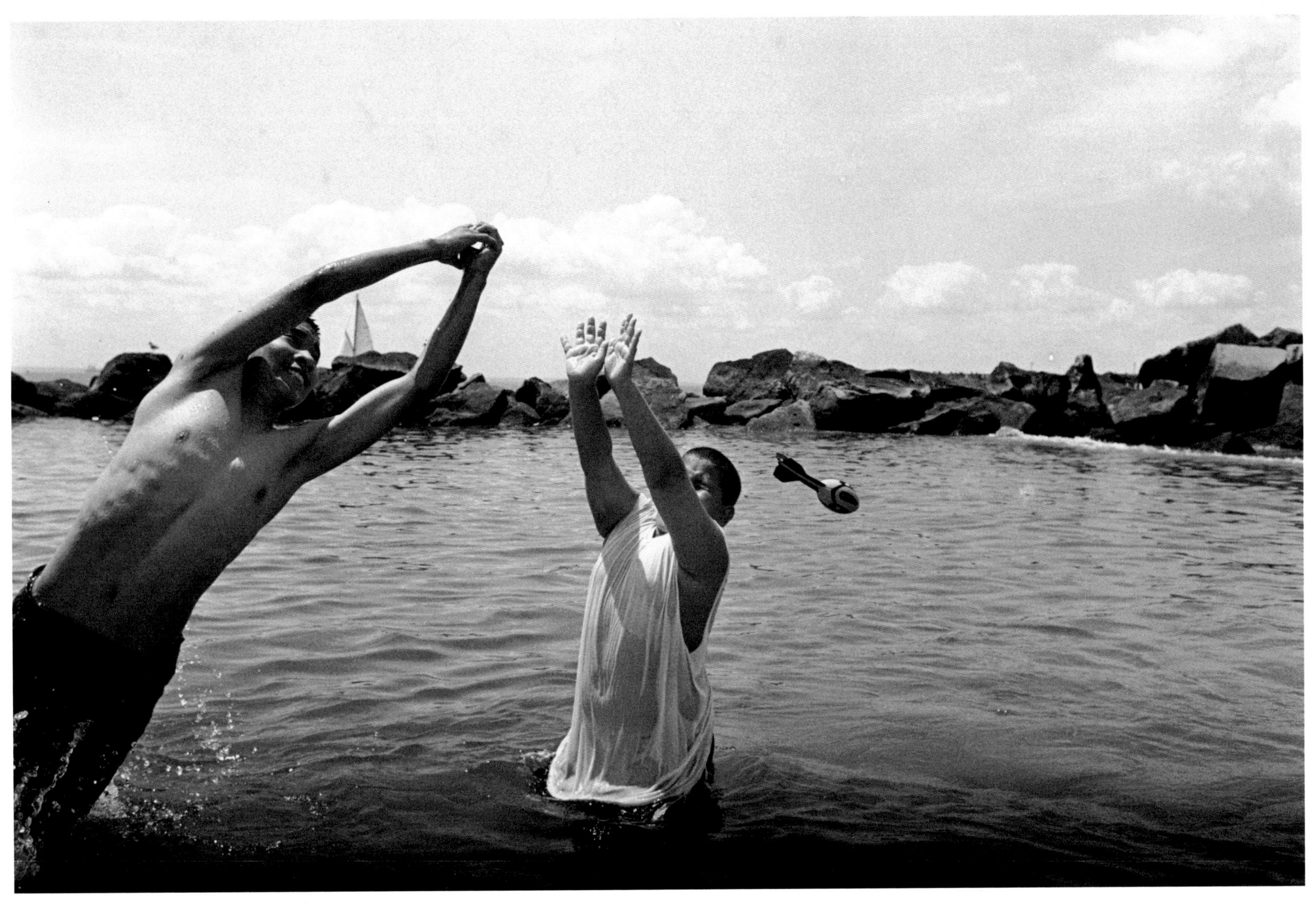

18.

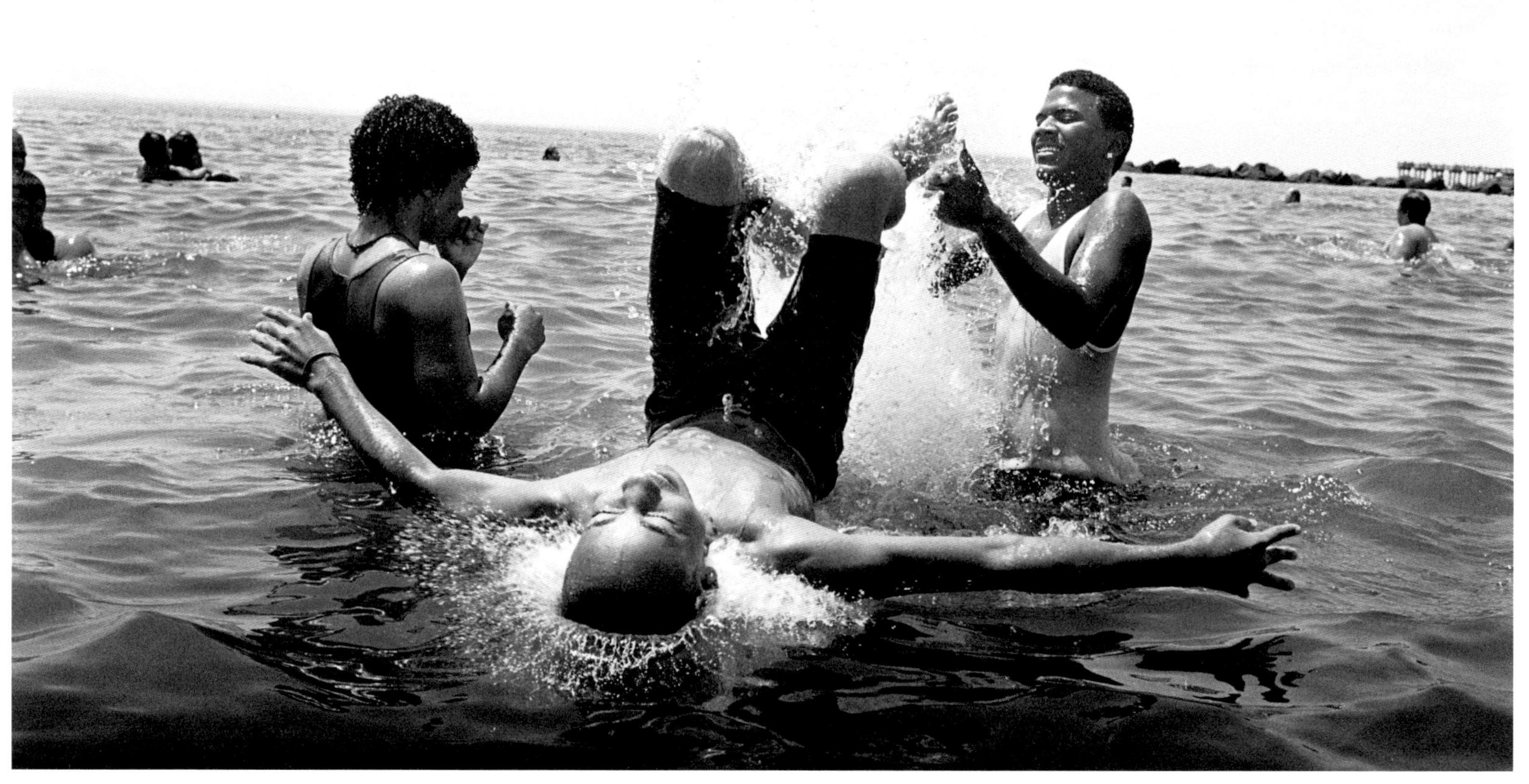

19.

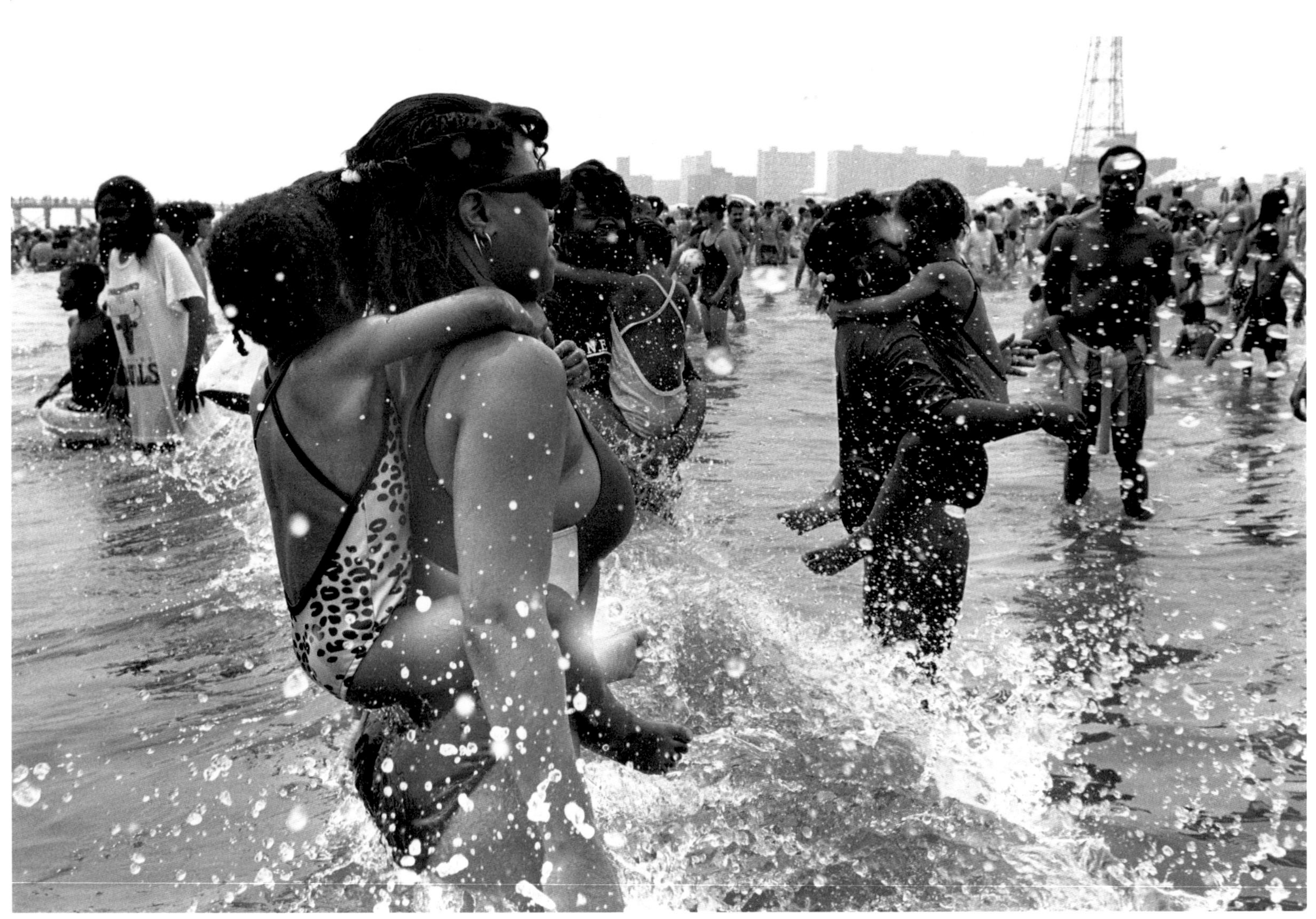

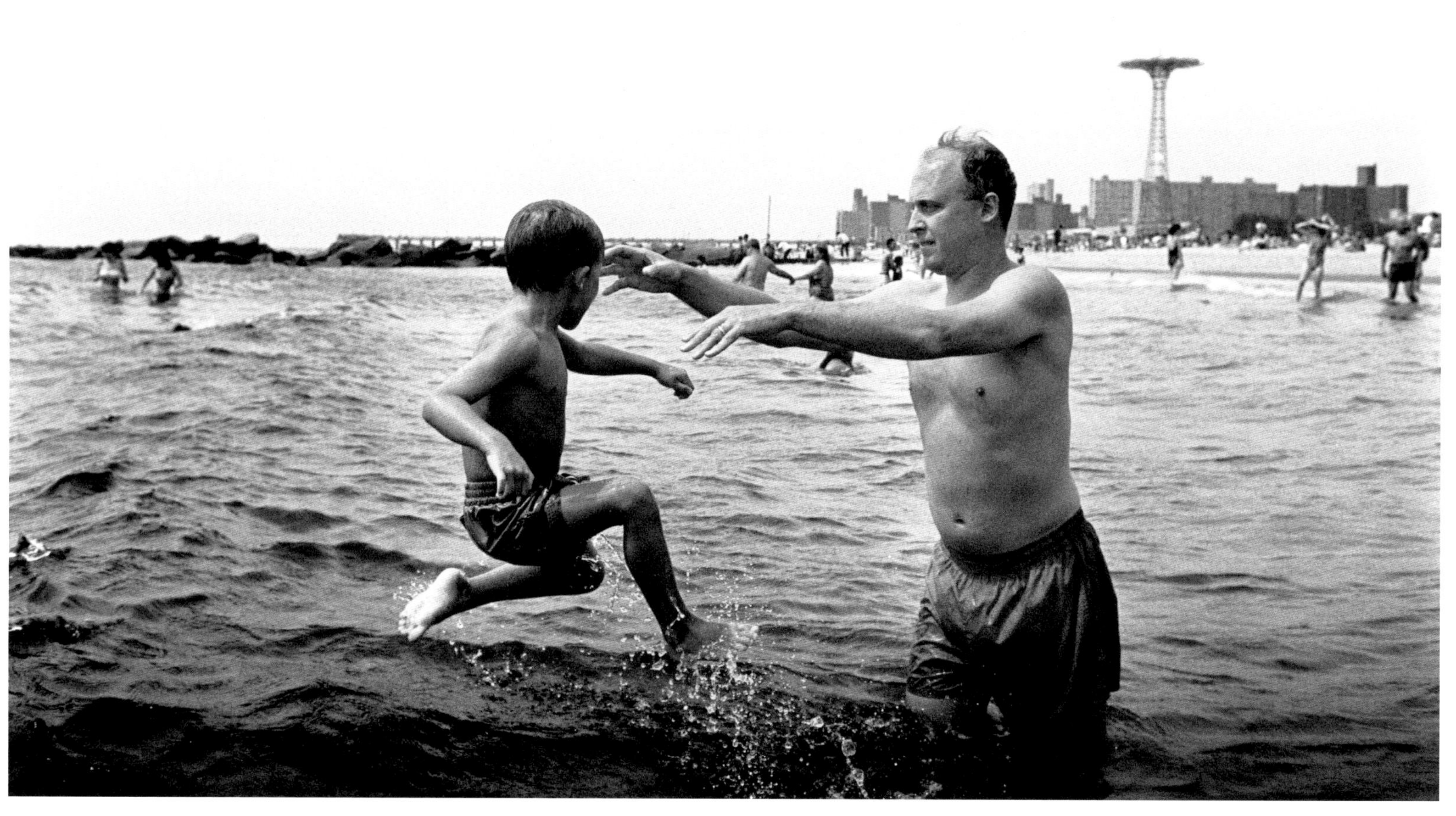

21.

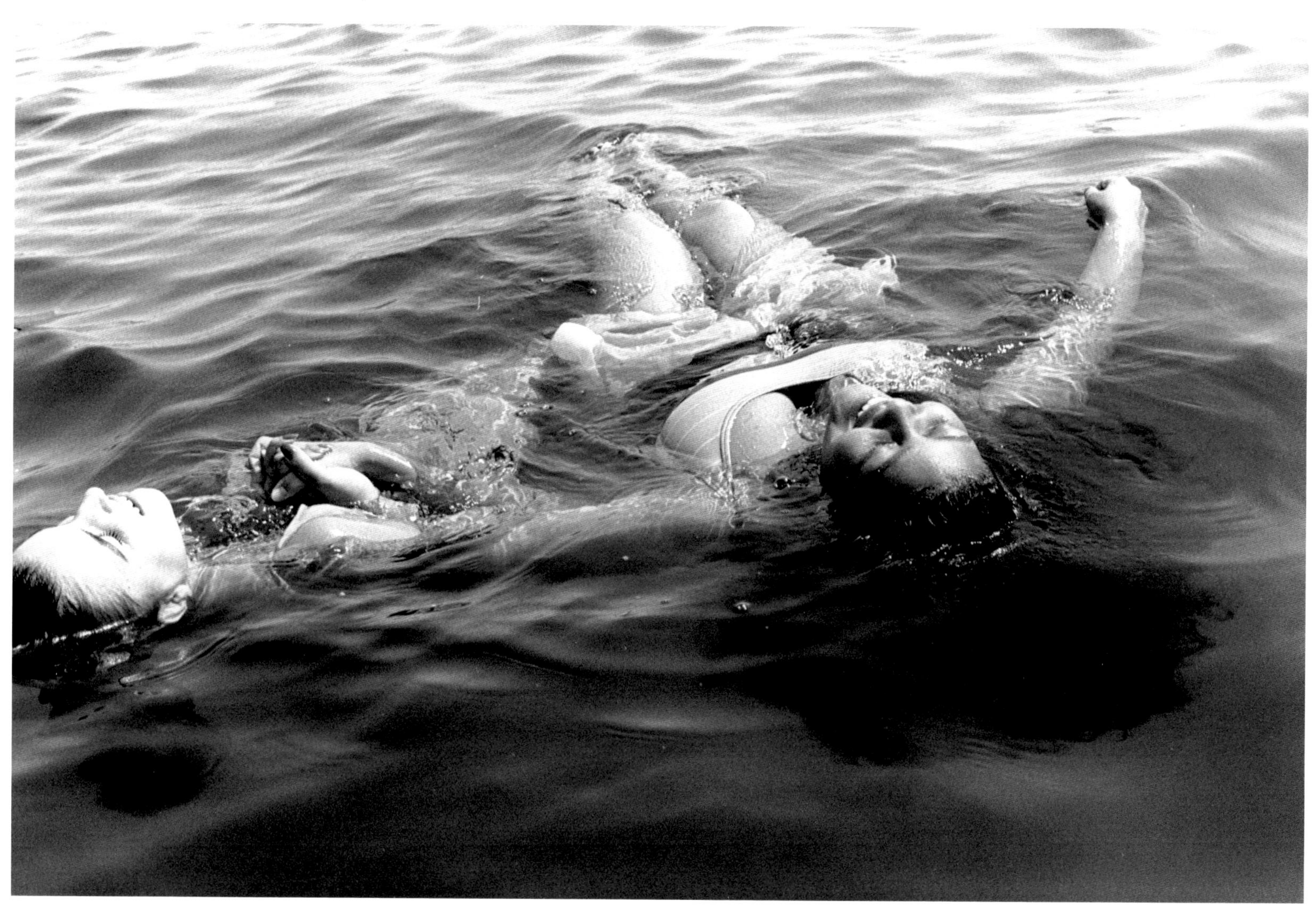

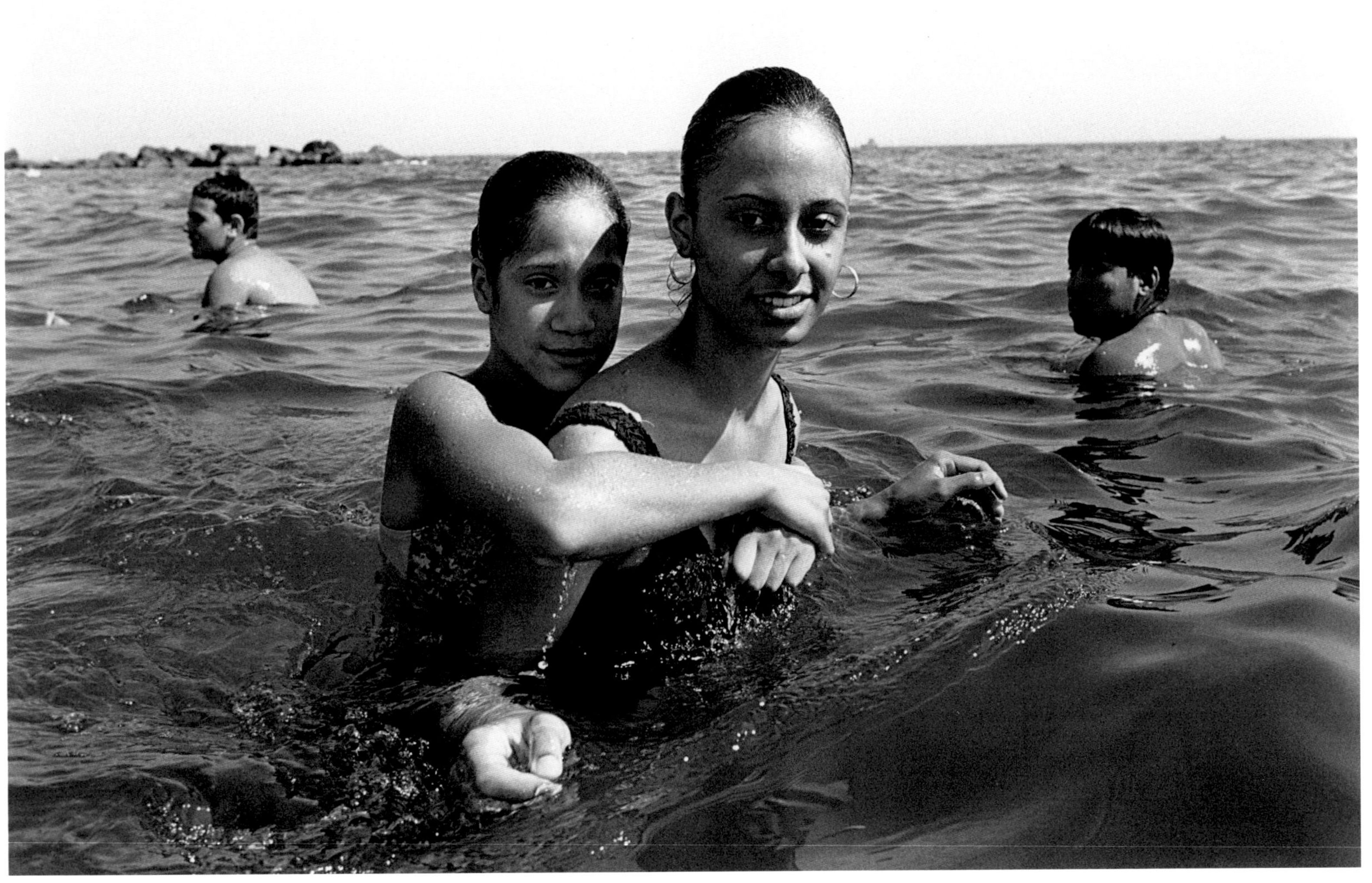

23.

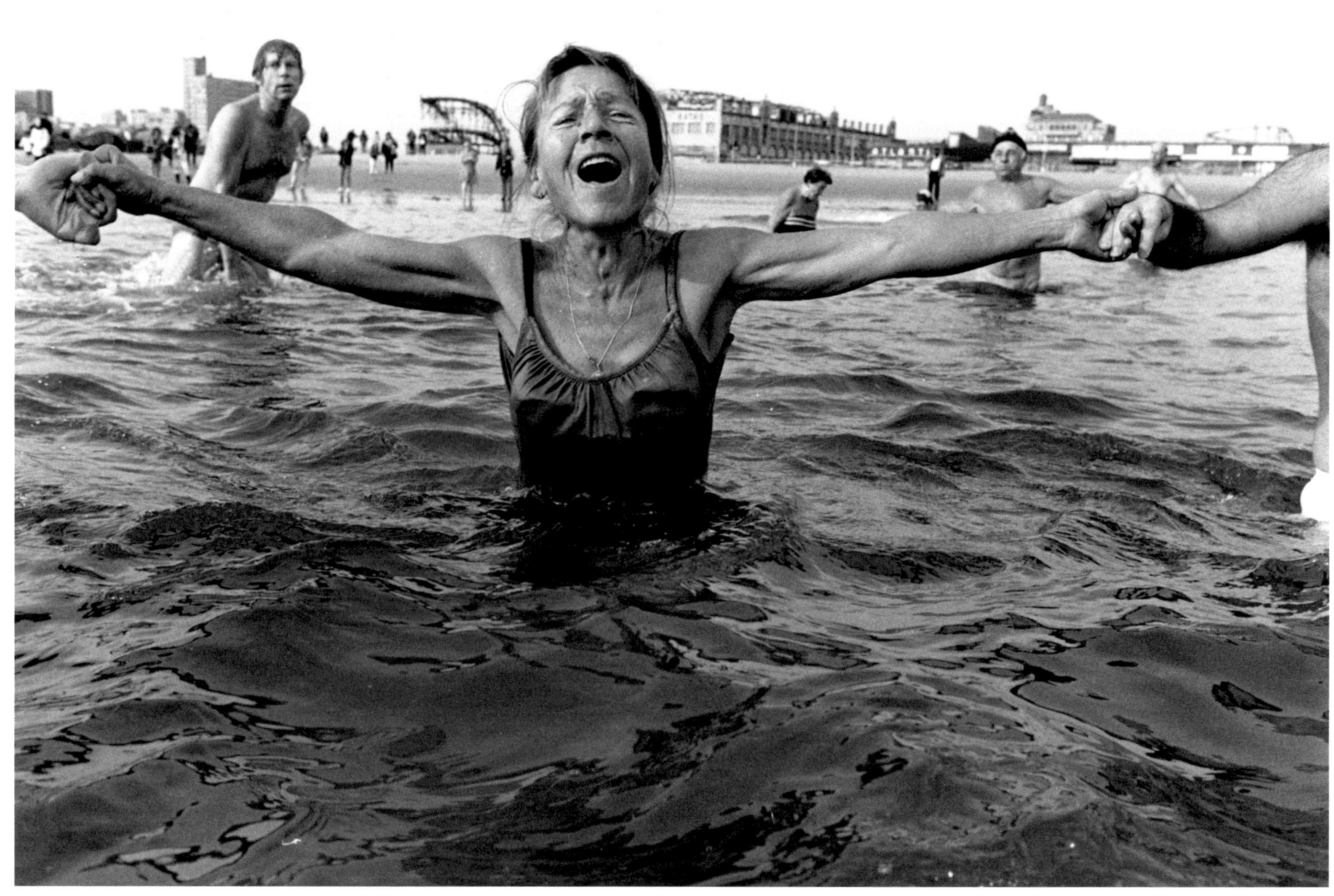

24.

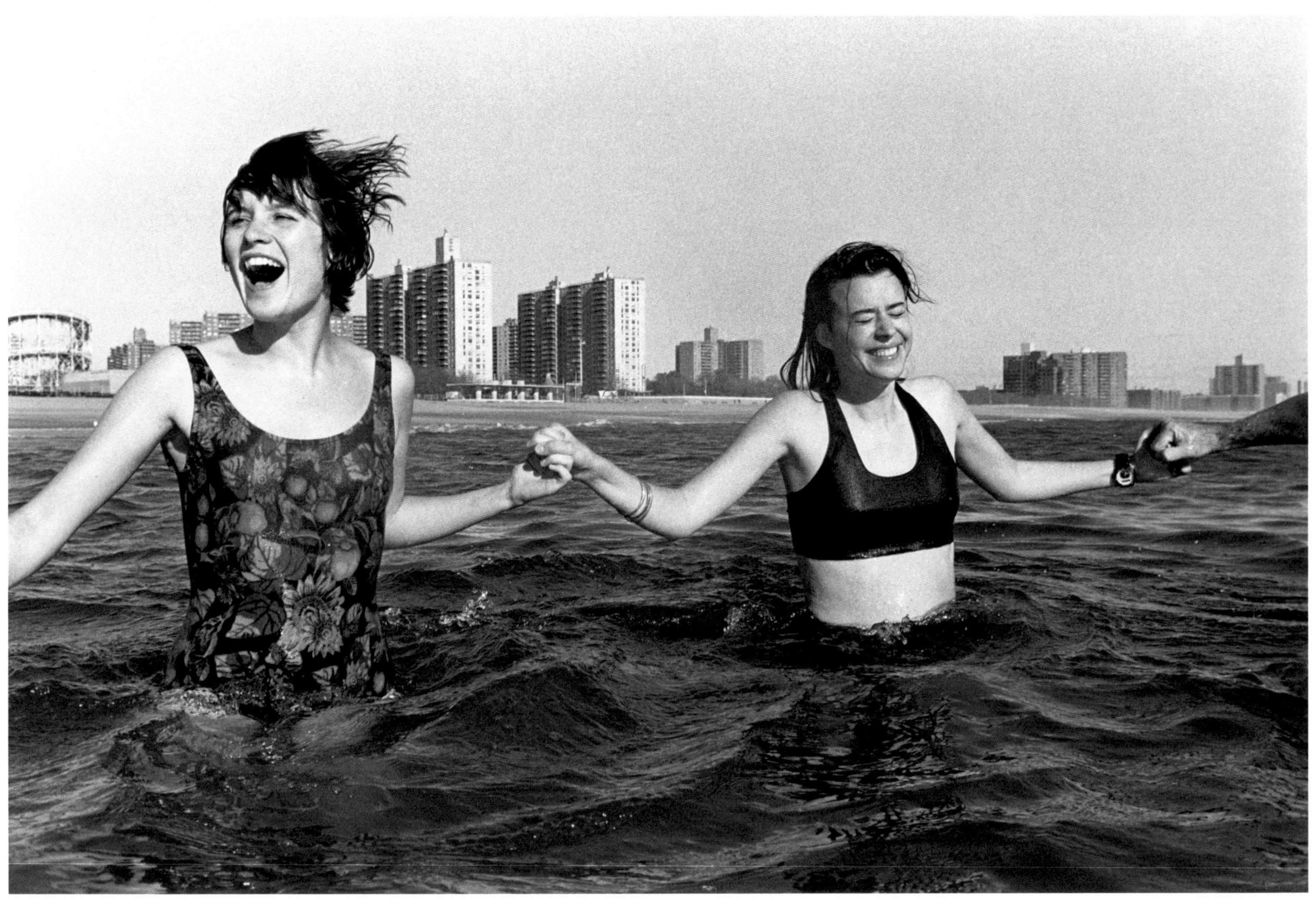

25.

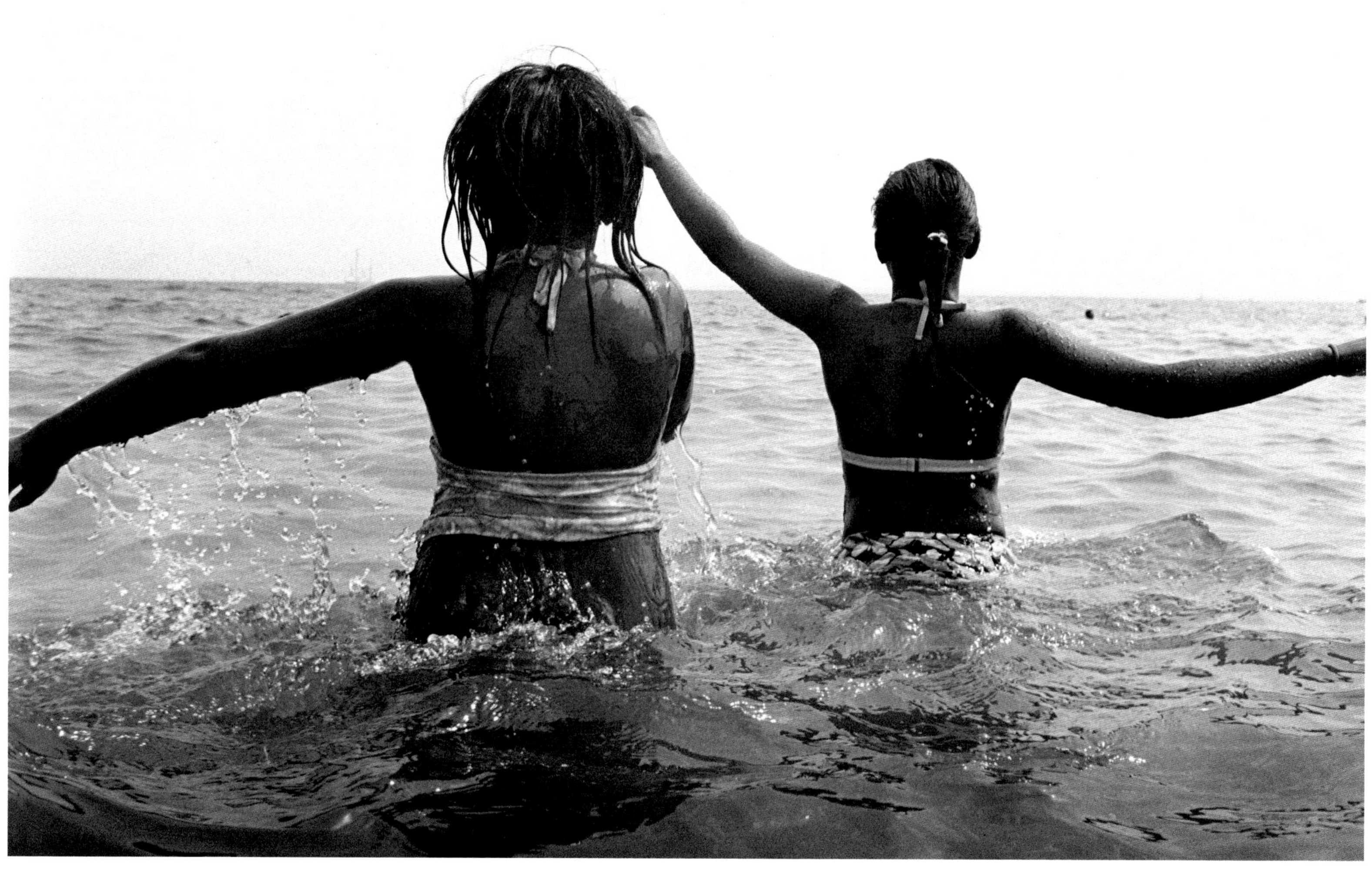

26.

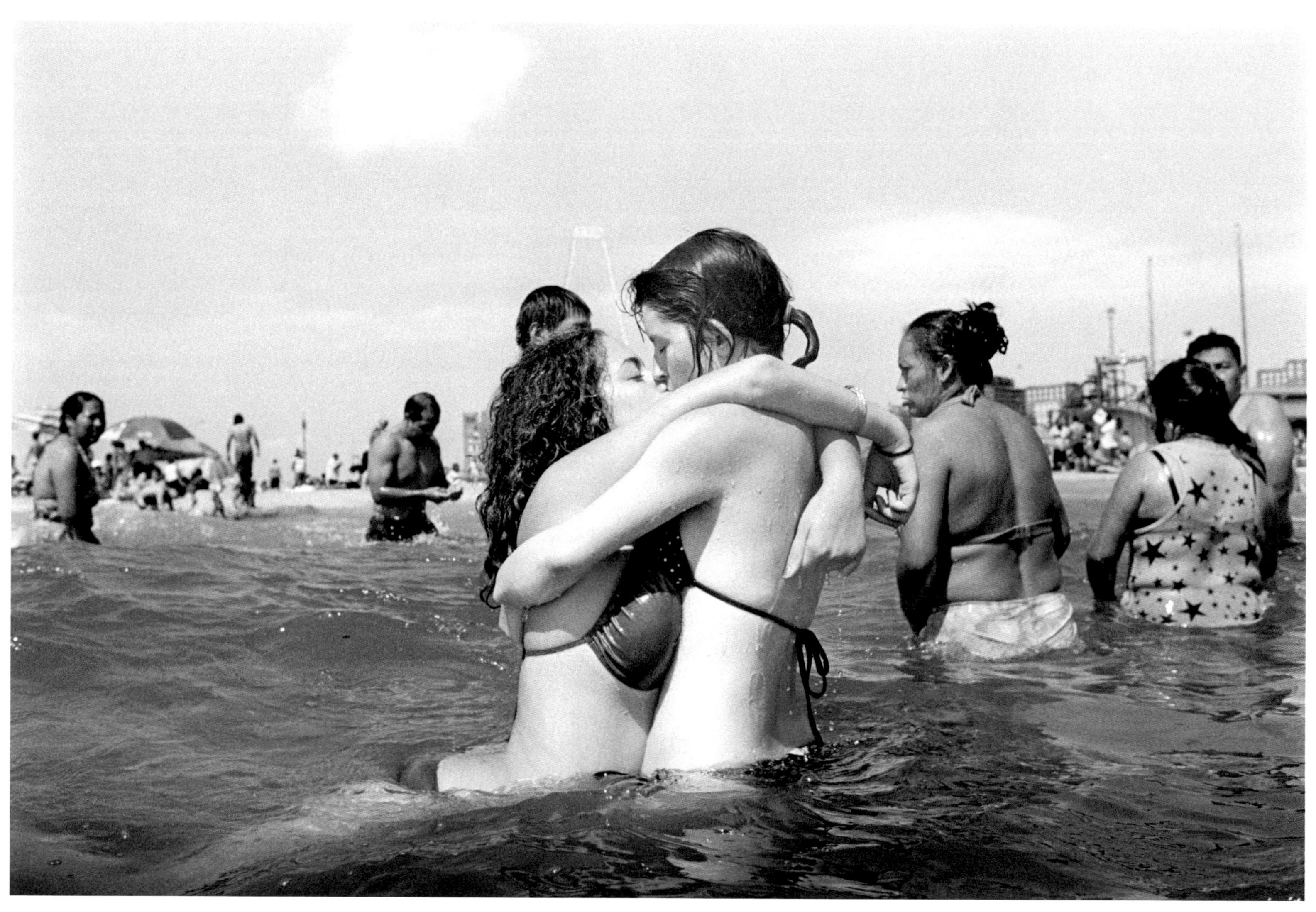

27.

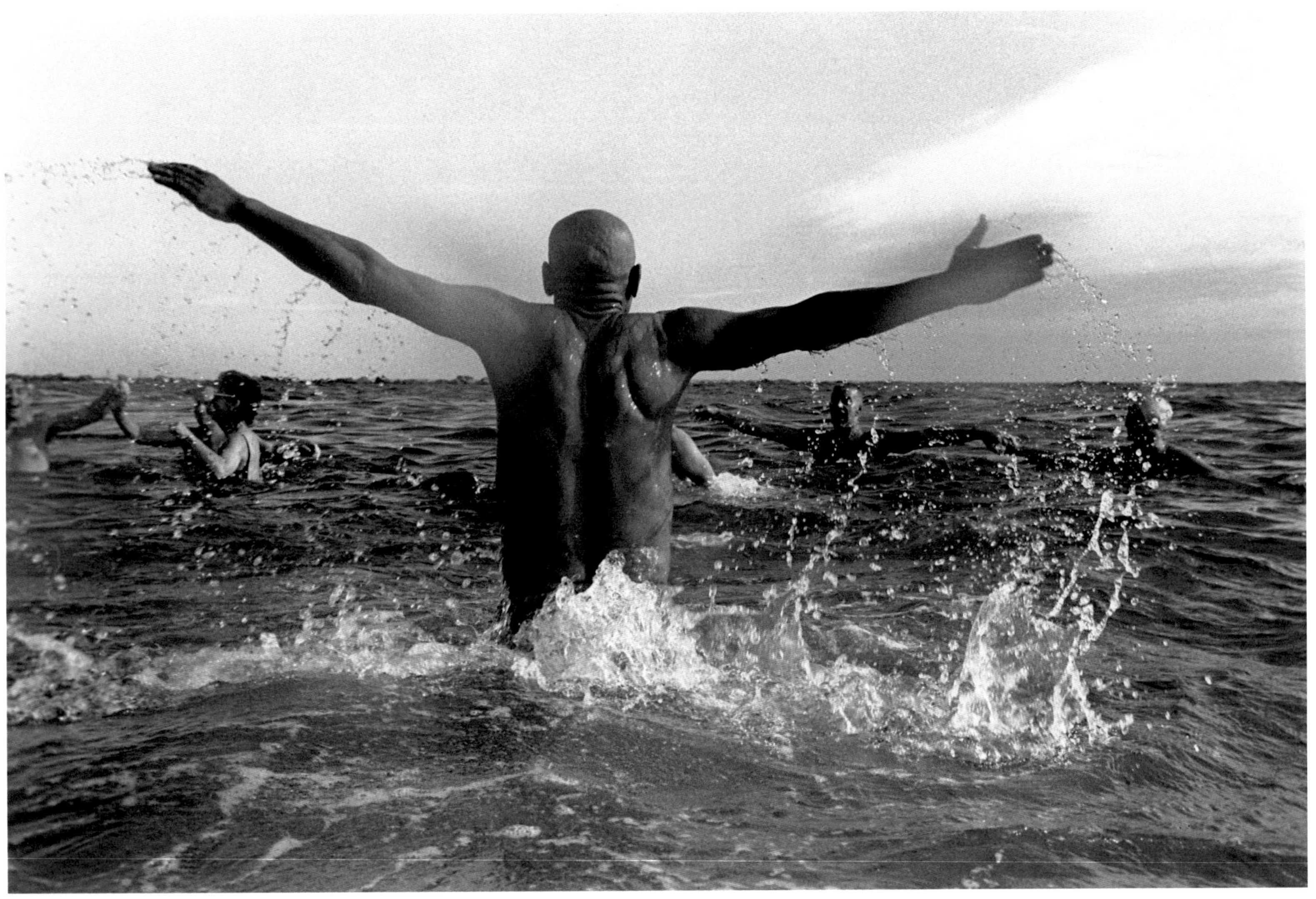

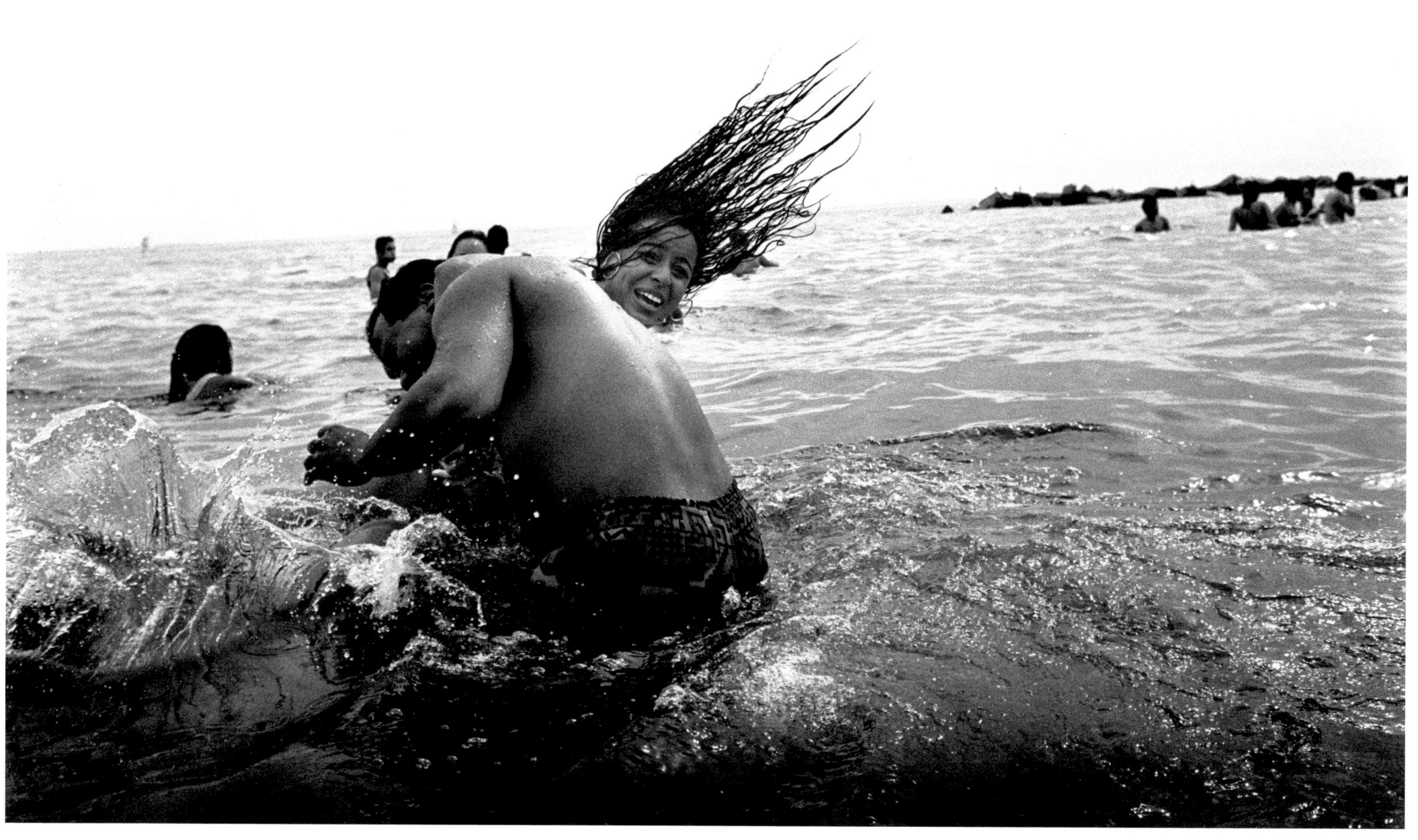

29.

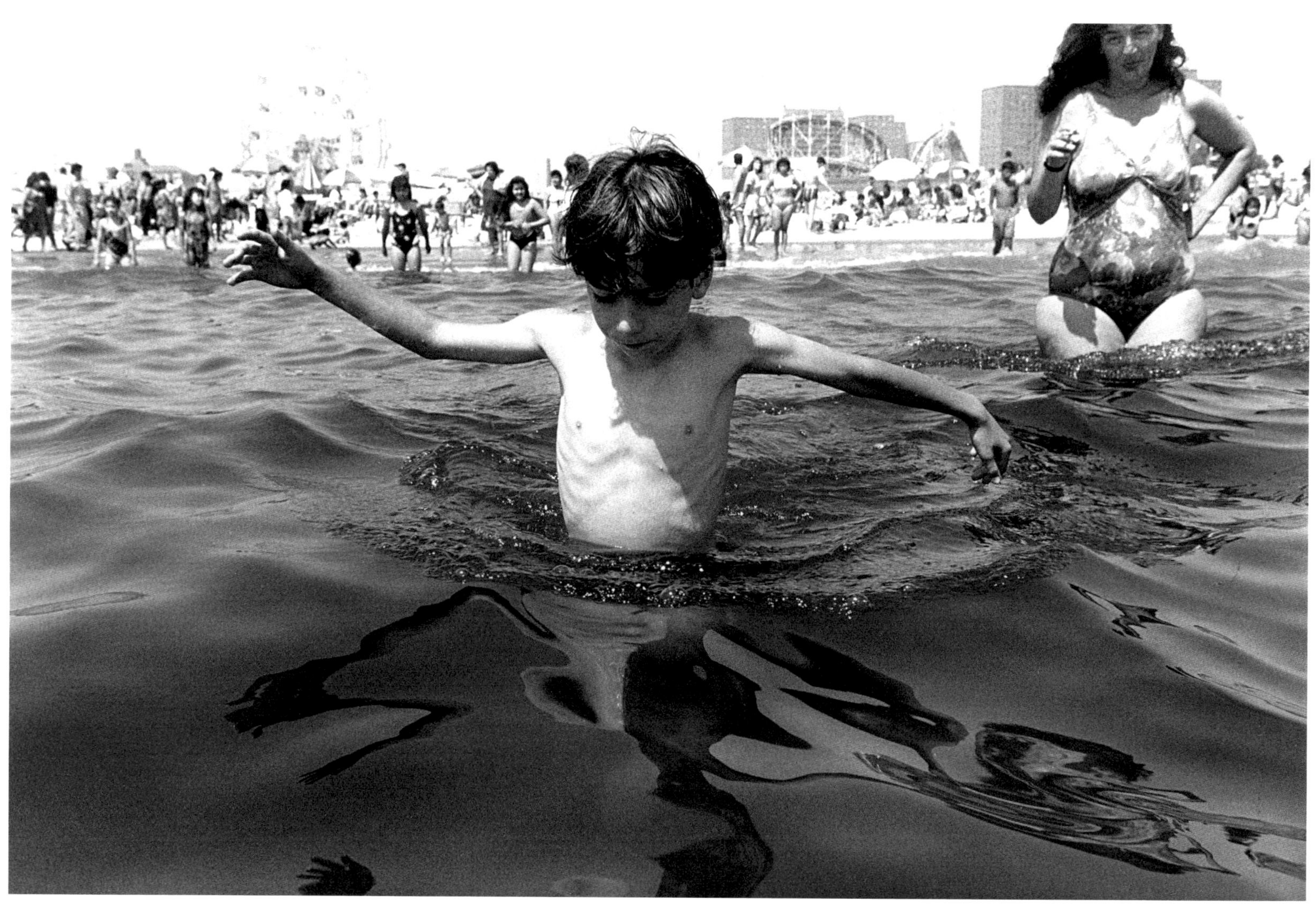

30.

DURING MY FIRST VISIT TO CONEY ISLAND, in the winter of 1990, I was standing on the boardwalk, bracing myself against the wind coming off the ocean, when a group of pink, half-naked men and women emerged from a cinderblock shed beneath my feet and quickly made their barefoot way across the snow-crusted sand toward the frigid ocean. After some jumping jacks, a bit of stretching, and a collective battle cry, they bounded into the water like lunatics out of the gate.

I guess I'd heard of the Polar Bear Club before, but their appearance in the flesh at that moment was a great surprise and delight. The next week, and each Sunday for the rest of that winter, I joined them with my waterproof Nikonos camera and a bathing suit. The club had been much photographed, but they told me I was the first photographer to suit up and join them in the water. I soon had a lot of new friends and a real appreciation for what that insanely cold water actually does to the body. It's true, as the Polar Bear Club claims, that the experience invigorates not only for the painful minutes while in the water but also for every day of the week to follow.

This experience is also how I fell in love with Coney Island. I photographed there regularly for two decades. The freak shows, the Mermaid Parade, the amusements, the boardwalk's old bars and games, the crowds on the beach—all were of great interest as subject matter to me. But it was the people in the water, in both winter and summer, that yielded the most satisfying photographs. I am most interested in the way people look when they don't know they are being photographed. The activity of being in the water, whether it is breathtakingly cold or welcome relief from summer heat, is both a distraction (good cover for a photographer) and a disinhibition, the combination of which makes for remarkably immediate, energized, and even intimate portraits. I kept my camera hidden underwater while I roamed through the crowds of people splashing, wrestling, or embracing; then, at the last moment, I pulled the camera up to my eye to make the photograph. These images are, for me, like passages from some primal, beautiful ballet—the energy, gesture, and emotion of the narrative rising and falling with the subjects on the waves.

—Peter Kayafas

Design and typography by Julie Fry
Printing by Studley Press,
    Suzanne Salinetti and Scott Artioli
Binding by Superior
Set in Bembo and Nobel